LET DANIEL SPEAK

LET DANIEL SPEAK

G. ARTHUR KEOUGH

REVIEW AND HERALD PUBLISHING ASSOCIATION
Washington, DC 20039-0555
Hagerstown, MD 21740

R&H Cataloging Service

Keough, George Arthur, 1909-
    Let Daniel speak.

        1. Bible. O.T. Daniel—Criticism, inter-
pretation, etc. I. Title.

                    224.5

ISBN 0-8280-0371-8

Dedicated

to the memory of

my parents

who,

by precept and example,

led me to accept the Bible

as the Word of God.

Contents

Introduction

Nothing can be more disturbing than to be in total ignorance about our origins, the purpose of living, and the destiny to which we may be headed. In order to face the future with confidence, we need to be certain about ourselves as human beings, about the God in whom we live and move and have our being, and about His eternal purposes. Can we really know these things?

I have written this book with the conviction that we have in the Bible a revelation that gives us adequate answers to all our questions. We need not wonder why we are here, where we came from, or where we are going. With adequate Bible study we can resolve our doubts and live our lives with understanding and confidence.

The Bible tells us that in the beginning God created the heavens and the earth. We have not arrived here by chance or accident. He created man in His own image, endowing us with the capacity to think and to do. And He created everything good. For God is good, God is kind, and everything He does is for our best interests. With such a Being in control of the universe, we have nothing to fear for ourselves or for the future.

Yet there is a fly in the ointment: we know that we are not perfect, and we recognize much that is wrong with the world in which we live. How did this come about? Again we are not left in the dark. The Bible tells us that though man was created perfect, he decided to disobey God, and sin entered into the world, and with sin came death.

Is the future, therefore, hopeless for us? No! God in His goodness gave humanity a second chance. He extended man's life and revealed a plan of salvation that would indicate without a doubt that He was not only good but extremely good and kind and loving. In God we have Someone in whom we can place our absolute trust.

In the story of Creation we have a record of God's absolute power. He speaks, and what He commands comes into being. "Let there be light," He said. And light, with all its mystery and power, burst into being. We cannot help but marvel at such creative ability. It is beyond our comprehension. But if God can do this, is there anything that can stand in His way?

But the Bible reveals another truth about God that boggles the mind: God can see into the future. We can stretch our imagination to understand how He can know all about the past. In the age of the computer we realize it is apparently a matter of memory capacity, although we must admit that this concept does not do justice to God's greatness and omniscience. We can even imagine how He would know about everything in the present, although in our extremely complex world such ability awes us! But can we conceive of God knowing everything that will happen in the future?

Can He see what has not yet taken place? If the universe were a machine, if man were an automaton, if everything were predetermined, we could comprehend how God could clearly see the future. But He has made us free moral agents. Heredity and environment do influence us, but in the major decisions of life, we must take responsibility for our actions. We recognize this when we are guilty and deserve to be punished. Also we know when we have done well and should be rewarded.

It is this matter of freedom of choice that makes it a marvel that God can see into the future without actually determining it. Some theologians do question the absolute foreknowledge of God. But the Bible tells us that God does know the future and has revealed it, and because of this, we can face the future with confidence.

The Bible is a whole library, but we will limit ourselves to a study of Daniel, a book in which we find prophecy and prediction. First of all, we will take up the phenomenon of prophecy in order that we may understand it in biblical terms. Then we will examine the book of Daniel chapter by chapter to see what God has revealed about the future and to learn how others have related to Him during trying circumstances. In this way we can know not only what we may expect but how we should respond to our varying circumstances. It is the conviction of the writer that in this way we can learn how to face the future with confidence and how to relate to the present in order to make that future a reality.

Basic Understandings and Presuppositions of the Author

I approach Daniel with the understanding that the book is a part of the canon of Scripture, and, therefore, I accept it as inspired by God. In the words of Paul, it is "God-breathed and is useful for teaching, rebuking, correcting and training in righteousness, so that the man of God may be thoroughly equipped for every good work" (2 Tim. 3:16, 17).

The Hebrew Bible places the book of Daniel in the third classification of the Holy Scriptures, the Writings, although the Septuagint, as do the English language versions, classifies it with the major prophets. There may be good reasons for the difference, but the matter of position does not alter the book's canonicity.

The Septuagint contains additions to the book of Daniel that the Hebrew lacks. These are: the prayer of Azariah in the furnace; the song of the three young men; the story of Susanna and the judgment of Daniel; and the story of Bel and the dragon. Since scholars recognize the passages as having been added after the completion of the Hebrew book, and because Protestants consider them apocryphal (they may be found as part of Scripture in Roman Catholic English versions), I have not dealt with them.

The book of Daniel is bilingual, part being in Hebrew and part in Aramaic. Scholars do not agree as to why this should be the case, but I accept the book as a unit, since there is strong evidence for its essential unity.

Because of increasing evidence of the historicity of Daniel, I have no hesitation in accepting the dating used in the book as valid indications of the historical background of the chapters.

Is the Book of Daniel Apocalyptic?

Scholars often classify the book of Daniel in the genre, or classification, of apocalyptic writing. "'Apocalypse' is a genre of revelatory literature with a narrative framework, in which a revelation is mediated by an otherworldly being to a human recipient, disclosing a transcendent reality that is both temporal, insofar as it envisages eschatological salvation, and spatial, insofar as it involves another, supernatural world" (from *Semeia 14*, p. 9, in John J. Collins, *Daniel: With an Introduction to Apocalyptic Literature* [Grand Rapids: William B. Eerdmans Pub. Co., 1984], p. 4).

In this sense we may refer to the book of Daniel and other parts of Scripture as apocalyptic. John J. Collins defines Daniel as "historical apocalypse" *(ibid.,* p. 6). The book certainly contains dreams and visions, has appearances of supernatural figures, and records angelic discourses.

However, many often regard apocalyptic writing as *ex eventu* prophecy, that is, history told in the form of prediction. This, we believe, is not true of the book of Daniel; abundant evidence exists that the book was authored by one who wrote autobiographically in the sixth century B.C. and who knew his contemporary history very well. To the conservative Christian, predictive prophecy is no theological problem. Hence we cannot classify the book of Daniel as apocalyptic if we must include the concept of a second century B.C. dating, with the name of Daniel being added pseudonymously.

How to Read the Book of Daniel With Maximum Profit

Remember that this is an inspired book and that only the Spirit that inspired the book in the first place can unlock its secrets. Pray for guidance and enlightenment in your study. Intelligence alone may lead to pride of opinion and dangerous misunderstanding. Read the book from every angle of history, geography, and literature. Bring every talent that you have to bear on the subject. With the right spirit you will be greatly rewarded.

Do not be discouraged or disappointed if you find differences of interpretation, even among the saints! It is always valuable to know when you can be dogmatic and when to reserve judgment. Share your insights with others who are wiser than you, and be guided by their criticism. Prophecy is not subject to private interpretation. Have an open mind to recognize fulfillment of prophecy, but do not be carried away by those who have bizarre interpretations and believe that they alone are right when the sound judgment of the church does not see eye-to-eye with them.

Finally, always refer back to the Scriptures. They alone, not the commentaries that others may write about them, are the source of truth.

The Value of the Study of the Book of Daniel

1. It reveals that God is active in history, that we are not left alone in this world to fend for ourselves. We may have our difficulties and trials, but we are not left subject to every whim and fancy of those around us. With God our lives can have meaning and direction.

2. It shows that God supports the righteous and punishes the wicked. We are not puppets of chance,

because when we choose to be with God, our destiny is secure.

3. It relates experiences that could well be repeated in our day. The book challenges young people to be like Daniel and his companions.

4. It assures us that God will destroy evil, even though He may, in order to reveal its true nature, allow it to pursue its wicked purposes for a time and appear to be victorious.

5. It promises the breakthrough of God's eternal kingdom of peace and righteousness, and with its appearance the triumph of all the righteous.

Acknowledgments

Among the many studies and books that the author has consulted in the preparation of this book, the following have been found particularly helpful:

Baldwin, Joyce. *Daniel: An Introduction and Commentary.* Downers Grove, Ill.: Inter-Varsity, 1978.

Ford, Desmond. *Daniel.* Nashville, Tenn.: Southern Pub. Assn., 1978.

Gaebelein, Frank E., ed. *Expositor's Bible Commentary: Daniel and the Minor Prophets.* Grand Rapids: Zondervan, 1985.

Maxwell, C. Mervyn. *God Cares: The Message of Daniel for You and Your Family.* Mountain View, Calif.: Pacific Press Pub. Assn., 1981.

Nichol, F. D., ed. *The Seventh-day Adventist Bible Commentary,* vol. 4. Washington, D.C.: Review and Herald Pub. Assn., 1977.

Shea, William H. *Selected Studies on Prophetic Interpretation.* Washington, D.C.: Review and Herald Pub. Assn., 1982.

Smith, Uriah. *The Prophecies of Daniel and Revelation.* Nashville, Tenn.: Southern Pub.

Assn., 1944.

White, Ellen G. *The Acts of the Apostles.* Mountain View, Calif.: Pacific Press Pub. Assn., 1911.

_____. *Education.* Mountain View, Calif.: Pacific Press Pub. Assn., 1952.

_____. *The Great Controversy.* Mountain View, Calif.: Pacific Press Pub. Assn., 1911.

_____. *Prophets and Kings.* Mountain View, Calif.: Pacific Press Pub. Assn., 1943.

Relevant articles by Arthur Ferch, Gerhard Hasel, William Shea, and others in *Andrews University Seminary Studies* were also relied upon.

Prophecy: God Communicates With Men Through Prophets

"All history proclaims, in one way or another, that there is a God ruling by His divine providence the various and perpetual moments of human affairs" (Pope Leo XIII).

Many Christians believe that God made the universe like one gigantic clock and has left it to run its predetermined course. In this case God is an absentee Landlord, and to pray to Him is futile. Prayer in such a situation only gives the one who prays a false sense of comfort or security—the comfort and security of one who whistles in the dark in order to allay his fears or to keep his spirits up!

The Bible, however, does not disclose that kind of God. On the contrary, it portrays Him as having always kept in touch with the human race and having revealed Himself supremely in Jesus of Nazareth. Far from neglecting the human race, God has always sought to guide and warn, and to make provision for man's eternal salvation.

God has used many ways to communicate with man. Occasionally He has spoken directly in what we call a theophany. Sometimes He has appeared in dreams and visions to indicate His purposes. But He has spoken largely through prophets, men and women whom He has called for a particular reason to give a certain message.

In this book we look at one of the greatest of the prophets, Daniel. He differs from most in the sense that he was more of a statesman than a preacher. Yet in his dedication to his task, he was also close to God, and God gave him insights important to him and to his contemporaries, and these have been recorded for the benefit of future generations. Although some scholars have doubted Daniel's authenticity and questioned the validity of his prophecies, many others accept the historicity of the book of Daniel and its place in the Bible. This book is written from this viewpoint.

Before we proceed with our study, it would be well to ask what prophecy is, what its purposes are, and how we can distinguish the true from the false.

What Is Prophecy?

Many view prophecy in terms of prediction. Thus *Webster's New World Dictionary* defines *prophecy* as "prediction of the future under the influence of divine guidance." However, the dictionary goes on to add: "act or practice of a prophet." In other words, prophecy means more than prediction—it includes the message of the prophet as a whole, which may be spoken, enacted, or written. Furthermore, it has a divine or supernatural source.

Thus prophecy is far from gazing into a crystal ball to satisfy idle curiosity regarding the future. It has nothing to do with magic or the study of the stars or witchcraft. Not of human making or initiative, it begins with God's initiative when He seeks to communicate with man.

This is not to deny that there may be false prophets and false prophecies. Sometimes we find more false prophets than true ones (1 John 4:1). Jesus warned His disciples against false prophets who come in sheep's clothing and yet are ravening wolves (Matt. 7:15). Such prophets would exist to the end of time (Matt. 24:11). It is important, therefore, to be able to distinguish the true from the false.

The true prophet will never contradict what Scripture has already revealed (1 John 4:2; Isa. 8:20). The false prophet will seek to add to Scripture or take away from it (Rev. 22:18, 19). Furthermore, if a prophet predicts an event that does not take place, then God has not spoken through him unless the prophecy is conditional. God has often warned of what will happen if people do not change their course of action. But when people repent and change their ways, then God alters the prediction to suit the new conditions (cf. Jonah).

Thus we see that prophecy is not merely to open up the future but to affect conduct in the present. It shows what the future has in store for those who follow a particular course of action. Prophecy seeks to discourage the wicked person from doing evil and to encourage the God-fearing individual to continue in the right way in order to enjoy the rewards that await him.

The Purpose of Prophecy

1. One goal of prophecy is to reveal the true God, because only the true God can reveal the future (Isa. 41:23, 26, 29).

2. Another is to show that God is concerned with what happens in history and that He can and will act accordingly to meet each situation (Gen. 6:5-8).

3. Prophecy reveals the standards by which God judges people (Prov. 14:34).

4. It lets people see that they are by no means the final arbiters of life. Everyone is accountable to a God in heaven, and it is the better part of wisdom to recognize the situation and act accordingly (Jer. 10:23; Prov. 3:6).

5. Because we are so prone to doubt, it helps to establish confidence and belief (John 14:29).

6. It gives hope for the future, telling the oppressed that a day of reckoning is coming when they will receive the reward of their faithfulness (Rom. 15:4).

Thus we see that prophecy, both in its predictive and informative aspects, has an important part to play in telling us what God seeks of us and what we may expect Him to do. It places us in the category of friends, rather than in the order of servants. God takes us into His confidence so that we can respond in an intelligent way to the varying circumstances in which we find ourselves. In the day of judgment none of us can say he did not know. We have no excuse for not being ready for any crisis, but every reason to believe the truth and to reject error in all its forms.

Problems With the Gift of Prophecy

Prophecy often employs symbols, but how can we interpret them with certainty?

Symbols may sometimes be difficult to interpret, but they are powerful in the sense that we can easily remember them. Like pictures, they remain in the mind when we have forgotten other aspects of the prophecy. We must be grateful for symbols and seek their interpretation in the Bible itself. If we find it there, we have no problem. We must let the same Spirit that gave the symbol interpret it for us. If, on the other hand, the Bible does not define it, we must not become dogmatic over its possible significance. At the same time we must avoid supposing that every aspect of a symbol has a meaning. Like a parable, a symbol has a primary focus, and we must not let secondary aspects dull our vision of the primary.

Another problem has to do with prediction. How can God see what has not yet happened?

Humanly speaking, this is an impossibility. Of course, we are all acquainted with the weather forecaster, who tells us what the weather is likely to be in the next few days. It is a standing joke that his forecasts are not likely to work out. No one blames him—it is impossible for him to know all the likely contingencies, even with the modern convenience of a computer! If we suppose that every cause has its corresponding effect and if we could only grasp all the causes at play, we could tell what the effects would be. Surely God knows all the factors in the present that would determine the future. But is this what we mean by prediction?

The above line of reasoning has one fatal flaw, and that is the assumption that everything in the universe works according to the laws of physics as we understand them. If we allow that man is not an automaton and that he is free to make choices that are not foreseeable, then we have a real problem with prediction, and we ask whether even God can foresee the unpredictable. Some theologians will argue that He does not know the future except in terms of what He plans to do or in general terms of what is likely to happen based upon the fact that He knows all the present and the past.

Most of us, I think, believe that God is all-knowing, and that means He knows the future as well as the present and the past. We may not understand how that can be, but then we do not understand many other aspects of the Godhead (1 Tim. 3:16). Perhaps our concept of time causes the difficulties. If God is the creator of time, then He cannot be bound by it. But to say this is only to emphasize the mystery!

The Wonder of Prophecy

When all is said and done, the wonder of prophecy is not so much that God can peer into the future and let us know what will happen; it is that God continues to communicate with man in spite of human waywardness and sin. When we think of how man never seems to learn his lesson, God's grace is boundless. We should not continue to presume on His goodness, but determine by His grace to search His Word, find out His will for us, and then do what we know ought to be done.

The Focal Point of Prophecy

If we study prophecy and never see Jesus Christ as the central focus of all history, the very hub of God's plan for human salvation, we have missed the most important element in revelation. Many prophets have existed during the history of the world, and Daniel was one of the greatest, but Jesus Christ was the prophet to whom Daniel pointed, the one who is the prophet par excellence! He termed Himself a prophet. The people called Him a prophet. His disciples recognized Him as a prophet. But He differed from all others in the sense that all human prophets delivered the word of God, but Jesus *was the Word.* Other prophets spoke the word from God, but Jesus was God speaking.

It is the prayer of the author that in the study of the book of Daniel, we shall not fail to see the "one like the Son of man" who was also the Son of God, and that knowing Him and His love for us, we shall always be able to face the future with confidence and understanding.

Principles of Prophetic Interpretation

We must approach the study of Scripture—particularly the prophetic parts of Scripture—with the understanding that the writers did not take up their pens and write according to their personal whims and fancies—the Holy Spirit (2 Peter 1:21) motivated them, and they wrote down and described what they believed was God's message, a divine revelation. We say that their writing is inspired by God and represents His word.

This being the case, Scripture carries with it an authority that is greater than any document produced by the human spirit. We can question the truth of a human author, we can wonder about his relevance for our own times, but we cannot doubt the truth or relevance of the canonical books of the Bible. That is why we study the book of Daniel—not to determine its veracity, but to discover its meaning. And the meaning is important for us because it is the word, not of man, but of God Himself.

As we study the prophetic parts of Scripture, we must have a knowledge of the languages and idioms used. In the case of translation, we must look at what a number of scholars have determined as the meaning of the original. We must have an acquaintance with the historical background of the writing, so that we can place it in its context. Further, we must be able to recognize literary allusions. And we cannot approach a particular part of the Bible without being aware of the thrust of the Bible as a whole.

Peter tells us that some distort Scripture (2 Peter 3:16) out of ignorance. They do not have the background to be able to relate new knowledge to the old. The apostle also describes them as unstable people, that is, those who are not firmly grounded in God's revelation and are easily drawn away by fanciful interpretations or even concepts of their own. Admittedly, some passages of Scripture are difficult to understand, but in such cases we must be careful not to jump to hasty conclusions.

In our study of Scripture we must not let personal views determine the meaning. Peter tells us that in the area of prophecy we must not let personal interpretations guide us (2 Peter 1:20). The same Spirit that prompted their composition in the first place must be the Spirit that provides the interpretation. Hence we need to be men and women of prayer, humbly seeking understanding. Intelligence alone will not lead us into truth. The Holy Spirit must illumine our minds if we are to grasp the import of the truths presented and to rightly interpret the symbols used.

We must recognize that false teachers exist today just as they did during ancient times. Not every interpretation is valid. We must be sure that the one we espouse is true to Scripture. That is why we should study the Bible itself and not what men may say about it. In addition, we must not add our own thoughts to Scripture or ignore any concepts it contains (Rev. 22:18, 19). We must be absolutely true to Scripture in our understanding of it.

As we mentioned previously, one of the problems posed by prophetic scripture is the use of symbols. When the context explains them, we have no problem. But sometimes the Bible writers employed symbols without interpreting them. In this case we should see whether the symbol appears in another part of the Bible. If so, then we have a clue. But when the Bible contains nothing to help us, then we can turn to someone recognized by the church as having the prophetic gift. Seventh-day Adventists are fortunate to have the writings of Ellen G. White, writings that have proved themselves to be in harmony with the teachings of the Bible.

And if her writings do not help us, then we must turn to dedicated Bible scholars who share with us their expertise in language and literature and background of history.

Finally, we must recognize that prophecy can be conditional (Jer. 18:5-11). At times a prediction may be postponed or set aside, as in the story of Jonah. We must be wary of a hard-and-fast interpretation that makes no allowances for variation or change. God is in charge, and He does what He sees is best in the circumstances. But does that mean that there is no certainty in prophecy? On the contrary, the vindication of the righteous and the destruction of the wicked is never in doubt. Time prophecies fulfilled to the letter assure us of the completion of other time prophecies. In reference to prophecies that yet await fulfillment, we must avoid dogmatism lest our expectations lead us astray. The Jews in the days of Christ permitted their interpretation of the work of the Messiah to lead them to reject the One who had come in fulfillment of prophecy.

Babylonian Exile: God Disciplines His People

"These things happened to them as examples and were written down as warnings for us, on whom the fulfillment of the ages has come" (1 Cor. 10:11).

A Crucial Event

Daniel begins his history with the year he and his companions went to Babylon as captives. In the reckoning of his time it was the third year of Jehoiakim, king of Judah, which corresponds to 605 B.C. in modern Western dating. Nebuchadnezzar had just inflicted a crushing defeat on the Egyptians at the Battle of Carchemish, and he proceeded to conquer all "Hatti country," that is, Syria and the territory to the south, including Judea, to the borders of Egypt. His progress halted when he heard of the death of his father, Nabopolassar, on August 16, and he took the shortest route home to succeed his father on September 7. Fortunately he found the Chaldeans in control in Babylon—his father being a Chaldean—and so his succession to the throne was assured. Meanwhile, Nebuchadnezzar had made arrangements to transport spoils and hostages from Jerusalem to Babylon.

Daniel adds a significant element to the story when he declares that it was God who had given Jehoiakim, king of Judah, into the hands of the Babylonian king. Here is a perspective on the event that we must not overlook. It tells us that God determined the result of the siege of Jerusalem.

It did not come about solely because of human activity. We are used to looking around us and attributing events to human factors such as greed, ambition, pride, and the desire to dominate. But according to the Bible, we make a mistake if we ignore the possibility of God's hand being active in the situations that affect our lives. From a humanistic perspective man is subject to the whims and fancies of those around him, but from the viewpoint of the Bible God is working out His plans and purposes, and He controls what may or may not be done.

Consternation in Jerusalem

The fall of Jerusalem must have come as a great shock to its inhabitants. It was not merely that they had suffered defeat, but their national pride had been hurt. Because of their conviction that they were God's people, they would naturally wonder, Where was God while all this was happening? With a sudden realization of tremendous loss, they would ask, "Has God forsaken us?" Citizen would ask citizen. Learned scholar would inquire of other learned scholars, "What has gone wrong?" It would be human to search for a scapegoat. Was the king to blame? Were the guards not on duty? And various answers would arise, but no one was really sure.

Perhaps the priests were the ones who were most scandalized. The Babylonians had taken or were given gold and silver vessels held for sacred use in the Temple. It was the ultimate in desecration. How could it happen? Why had God not struck anyone dead? The event was seemingly inexplicable.

The members of the royal family were at a loss to explain their defeat. They could not understand how a pagan king had met with such success against a city that God had chosen, with a temple where its people worshiped God in forms and ceremonies handed down from the days of Moses. Furthermore, they had to say goodbye to some of the brightest of their youth. What was going to happen next?

No doubt every citizen, every household, had offered fervent prayers, pleading with God to save the city. No one wanted to see such an upheaval. Yet the unexpected had happened. Where was God? Did He not hear and answer His people anymore? Anyone who has experienced a tragedy in his life can enter into the feelings and questionings of the Jews in Jerusalem at that time.

The Perspective of History

Some wise men in Jerusalem could refer to their scrolls, could dig into their history and see if there were any lessons to learn from their past experience.

The story of Hezekiah provided one example (2 Kings 20:1-11). King of Judah, he had been extremely sick, but he did not want to die. Although God had told him through the prophet Isaiah to order his affairs because he would die, he pleaded for life and healing; and God did a surprising thing: He apparently changed His mind!

Here is an important insight into God's character. He cares for His people. The Lord knows what is best for them and warns them accordingly. But when His people ask for mercy and grace, He allows for changes in plans if by any means He can secure their gratitude and devotion. All His plans are in man's favor.

In Hezekiah's case God did more than heal the king and give him an extra lease on life. He gave him a sign, that of shifting the shadow on the sundial. The miracle not only assured Hezekiah that He would keep His word, but showed him and everyone else that God is in control of everything and that He can do anything He pleases. Do we recognize God's sovereignty in everything?

The tragedy in Hezekiah's story is that the king failed to give God the glory for his healing and life. When visitors arrived from Babylon, impressed by the phenomenon of the retreating sundial shadow—for the Babylonians were great astronomers—Hezekiah breathed no word about God's love and power. Instead of witnessing to what should have been his faith, he gave his visitors a conducted tour of his storehouses, of his silver and gold, his armory, and the glories of his kingdom (verses 12, 13). The incident clearly indicated his priorities.

God's response was swift and sure. Through the prophet, Hezekiah was to hear the word of God: "The time will surely come when everything in your palace, and all that your fathers have stored up until this day, will be carried off to Babylon. . . . And some of your descendants, your own flesh and blood, . . . will be taken away, and they will become eunuchs in the palace of the king of Babylon" (versus 17, 18).

Here was a clear statement of what would have to happen if the kings of Judah had their priorities upside down. One can imagine the sages in Jerusalem nodding their heads with understanding as they read the scrolls. God is a God of mercy, but He is also a God of justice (Ex. 20:5, 6). They would see that when the leaders of Judah set the wrong example and the people follow suit, they can expect nothing but the fulfillment of God's warning.

As the sages read on in the scrolls, they would learn about Hezekiah's son Manasseh. Unfortunately the son was not like his father in terms of being a reformer (2 Kings 18:1-4). He reflected his father's concern for the temporal rather than the spiritual. Manasseh reverted to the evil practices of the surrounding nations. God is slow to anger (Neh. 9:17), but Scripture tells us that Manasseh provoked Him to anger (2 Kings 21:6).

We are not surprised at the divine reaction when we read all that he did, including sacrificing his son in the fire (verses 3-6). Tradition has it that he sawed the prophet Isaiah in half between two planks of wood (see *Prophets and Kings*, p. 382). God responded by declaring that He would bring "such disaster on Jerusalem and Judah that the ears of everyone who hears of it will tingle" (verse 12). God used a striking metaphor when He said, "I will wipe out Jerusalem as one wipes a dish, wiping it and turning it upside down" (verse

13). In spite of the warning, Manasseh and his people paid no attention, and the chronicler records, "So the Lord brought against them the army commanders of the king of Assyria, who took Manasseh prisoner, put a hook in his nose, bound him with bronze shackles and took him to Babylon" (2 Chron. 33:11).

God shows His mercy when Manasseh repented and humbled himself by bringing him back to Jerusalem. "Then Manasseh knew that the Lord is God" (verse 13). But Manasseh's son was not any better. It was fortunate that he reigned only two years (2 Kings 21:19-23). Then a change of situation arose when Ammon's son ascended the throne. Josiah is an example of how the son does not have to follow the evil behavior of a father. "He did what was right in the eyes of the Lord and walked in all the ways of his father David, not turning aside to the right or to the left" (2 Kings 22:2).

Repairs in the Temple led to the discovery of the book of the Law. Reading the scroll produced deep concern and repentance. Therefore God sent an encouraging word to Josiah, telling him that while He had not changed as far as the matter of disaster on Jerusalem was concerned, it would not come in his days. "Your eyes will not see all the disaster I am going to bring on this place" (verse 20). Once again we see God's long-suffering mercy. We also observe that the path of blessing depends on a faithful obedience to God's injunctions.

Calamity in the Days of Jehoiakim

The behavior of the kings of Judah is a sad story, and Jehoiakim proved no better than his wicked predecessors. It is not surprising, therefore, that calamity would strike in his days. But not without warning. For 23 years Jeremiah had issued his appeals again and again. But no one would listen (Jer. 25:3). God said, "I will summon all the peoples of the north and my servant Nebuchadnezzar king of Babylon, . . . and I will bring them against this land and its inhabitants and against all the surrounding nations. I will completely destroy them and make them an object of horror and scorn, and an everlasting ruin" (verse 9). The only note of relief was that the captivity would last only 70 years (verse 11).

Hebrew Youths

Several youths living in Jerusalem at this time no doubt watched events with great interest and concern. Daniel may well have been about 18 years of age when taken captive. He was old enough to be well versed in Scripture, to have learned a good deal about the history of his people, and to distinguish between truth and error. It is reasonable to assume that he and his companions were idealistic, would regret the evil that was done, and would like to see a reform. But they were not old enough to effect one.

Daniel does not complain about his fate. Doubtless he could see that the innocent suffered with the guilty. But that is a fact of life. We cannot deny that we are part of the human family. Often we are tempted to ask, "Why me?" But we brush the question aside as inconsequential, continuing to live our lives under God, knowing that it is our duty to do what is right regardless of what may be happening to others. We believe that God will provide what is best for us individually, whether we understand the situation or not. It is this faith and confidence that makes life worth living.

The Hebrew captive revealed an important philosophy of life soon after he arrived in Babylon. He did not object to receiving a new name, although it contained the name of a pagan god. Some matters are important, but others are not worth a fight. Thus he saw no religious principle involved in the use of a Babylonian name. Nor did he refuse to study the Babylonian language and literature, although he must have known that it would contain erroneous human sentiments. If his knowledge of the language and literature of his captors would enable him to understand them better and to witness to them more effectively, then he saw some advantage in such study. Knowing the Scriptures as he did, he would be better able to distinguish between truth and error. Furthermore, it had not been his choice to study at the University of Babylon. It was part of a providential plan for him.

But Daniel determined that he would not defile himself with the food and wine provided by the king (Dan. 1:8). As a devout Jew, he took this position for a number of reasons:

1. He would not want to eat meat considered unclean and unfit for human consumption according to Levitical law (Lev. 11).

2. He would not want to eat flesh first offered to idols, because in so doing he would seem to be participating in a pagan religious practice.

3. He would not want to eat meat not slaughtered according to Jewish practice, because it would still have the blood of the animal in it (Lev. 17:13, 14).

4. He would not want to jeopardize his health by indulging in a diet that would be rich in condiments and spices, combined in a manner that would put a heavy strain on his digestive system. Daniel felt that it was his religious duty to conserve his strength for the service of God.

5. He would remember the injunction of the wise man regarding wine and would abstain from anything that would impair his judgment (Prov. 20:1; 23:31, 32).

6. Finally, he would remember that to accept patronage from a ruler restricts one's independence. It always pays to not be obligated to anyone (Prov. 23:1-3).

Probably Daniel saw through Nebuchadnezzar's policy of treating hostages with favor. He felt sure that the king knew he could not bring about change immediately, but with kindness he might ease the road to compromise. Thus Daniel saw that it was essential, at the very beginning, to keep clear of all possible entanglement.

Tact and Divine Favor

Daniel tells us how he sought to persuade the authorities to grant an exception in his case. He approached the one in charge with his request, and when the official politely refused the petition on the grounds that to do so would endanger his life and position, Daniel did not pursue the matter any further lest he cause resentment. But he did not give up. He went to the person second in command with a suggestion so reasonable that the man could hardly refuse it. And Daniel won his case. He received permission to test a simple diet—consisting mainly of vegetables—for 10 days; and if he seemed to thrive on it, it could continue. We all know the story. He proved that a simple diet was more conducive to health than a rich one.

But Daniel makes it clear that divine favor accompanied his successful use of tact. When the human and the divine cooperate, miracles can happen. Daniel's superiors had confidence in him and were willing to help him out in any way they could because they recognized in him one who was honest, dependable, and eager to please. He did not try to curry favor, nor did he adopt the sullen stance of a captive. His superiors appreciated his hard and willing service.

The Secret of Success

The Hebrew youth proved to be a good student, but he attributed his success not to his native intelligence but to a gift from God. It was God who gave him knowledge and skill and understanding. Because Daniel recognized the source of all true success and decided to be faithful to his God, He could abundantly bless him. At the same time the young man was diligent in his work and tactful in his relations with others, so that his witness for God was supremely effective.

Although Daniel exemplified principles that lead to success, we must not suppose that a mechanical application of them will always have the desired result. The Christian must be prepared to meet opposition and sometimes even failure. In addition, it is difficult to measure true success. Only in eternity will we know the true results of our efforts.

Graduation With Honors

Daniel and his companions did well in their studies. The Babylonians enrolled them in a course that was to take three years, but it probably involved one full year and parts of two others. If they began their studies as soon as they arrived in Babylon, in the accession year of King Nebuchadnezzar, they would have completed them in the second year of the king's reign. (This is a common method of reckoning in Bible times and countries.)

When Nebuchadnezzar participated in the final examinations, he saw with his own eyes and heard with his own ears the outstanding skill of the captives from Judah. It speaks well for him that he promoted people to high office on the basis of talent and not because of race or nationality.

Daniel served in high office for more than 70 years. He began in the reign of Nebuchadnezzar and continued till the rulership of Cyrus. God wonderfully blessed His dedicated servant.

PRINCIPLES OF LIFE

The following propositions are for your consideration. Do you agree that they offer valid biblical principles by which to guide our lives?

1. To live according to God's laws is to enjoy a life of challenge and satisfaction.

2. To ignore His teaching and to go one's own way is to court disaster.

3. Because God knows best whether we should live or die, we should be willing to accept His plans, however different they may be from our own.

4. God often mercifully shields us from the consequences of our own acts, but the time comes when we must face discipline.

5. The object of His discipline is to secure repentance and conversion.

LDS-3

6. Man has no excuse for not knowing God's will or the reward of rightdoing. He has given us abundant evidence in His Word and in history.

7. Happy is the man who determines to do what is right regardless of the consequences. God is on his side and will give him all the help he needs.

8. The laws of health are as sacred as those of true worship.

9. True success is measured by one's dedication to God and acceptance of His plan for our lives.

WORTH NOTING:

"While Daniel clung to God with unwavering trust, the spirit of prophetic power came upon him. While honored by men with the responsibilities of the court and the secrets of the kingdom, he was honored by God as His ambassador, and taught to read the mysteries of ages to come" *(Education,* p. 56).

"The history of Joseph and Daniel is an illustration of what He will do for those who yield themselves to Him and with the whole heart seek to accomplish His purpose" *(ibid.,* p. 57).

"Every youth, every child, has a work to do for the honor of God and the uplifting of humanity" *(ibid.,* p. 58).

The Goal of History: God's Eternal Kingdom

"In the annals of human history the growth of nations, the rise and fall of empires, appear as dependent on the will and prowess of man. The shaping of events seems, to a great degree, to be determined by his power, ambition, or caprice. But in the word of God the curtain is drawn aside, and we behold, behind, above, and through all the play and counterplay of human interests and power and passions, the agencies of the all-merciful One, silently, patiently working out the counsels of His own will" (Education, p. 173).

Without necessarily thinking of what the statement implies, we often say that history repeats itself. Of course, some believe history goes in circles; others may add the concept of advancing upward in spirals. But the Bible knows only one kind of history, that which has a beginning and proceeds to a predetermined end—the destruction of evil and the restoration of God's eternal kingdom of peace and righteousness.

We do not know what Nebuchadnezzar's thoughts may have been in regard to history, but we may be sure that he was anxious to establish himself firmly on the throne and to ensure his dynasty for a long time to come. This was only human. Also we know that he was an intelligent man and a great leader.

The Babylonian chronicle, some of the tablets that archeologists have discovered and read, tells of Nebuchadnezzar's success in leading his armies to victory, in bringing opposing rulers to their knees in submission, in carrying back to Babylon large quantities of booty, and in undertaking great plans for rebuilding and beautifying his capital city. For instance, we know that he ordered for his wife the construction of the Hanging Gardens, which the Greeks later described as one of the seven wonders of the world.

Did he, perchance, stop to wonder whether the empire he was building would last forever? Did he wonder whether his officers would remain loyal to him? He knew how he and his father had overthrown the Assyrian empire. Did he question the tenets of the Babylonian religion, the authority of the priests, the so-called prowess of the gods?

The Bible emphasizes that there is only one true God. The gods that men set up are but figments of the imagination, and to worship them is worse than useless. Man needs assurance that the God of heaven created us and is interested in our eternal welfare. He plays an active part in history and has always communicated with man, from Adam to Noah to Abraham to the kings of Israel. The only question would be: Would God communicate directly with a ruler like Nebuchadnezzar?

Daniel tells us that He did in a dream, an approach that Nebuchadnezzar would understand. Babylonians believed that the gods communicated with men through such dreams. They had literature that explained all about dreams and what they could mean. All they needed to know was the dream, and then they could research the interpretation.

Nebuchadnezzar was well aware of this. God's part was to give him a dream, to have him feel that he should not ignore it, and then to make him hazy about the details so that he would not be able to recall it satisfactorily. In this way the wise men of Babylon would not be able to pretend to give an interpretation.

The morning afterward the king did what he would be expected to do: He called in all the experts around his palace, all those who might be able to unravel the dream.

Daniel names them as magicians, astrologers, sorcerers, and Chaldeans (see Dan. 2:2, KJV). Scripture condemns many of these practices.

Thus we read of magicians in Egypt who could do wonders with their "secret arts" (Ex. 8:7). But they were limited in what they could do. They had to admit before Pharaoh that what Moses and Aaron accomplished by the power of God in the plague of gnats was beyond their capability (verses 18, 19). Sometimes they were not able to interpret a dream (Gen. 41:8, 24).

Astrologers claimed to foretell the future by studying the relative position of stars and planets. They accompanied a king or ruler wherever he went and advised him as to propitious or unpropitious times for undertakings.

Sorcerers used enchantments and magic spells. They were mediums and spiritists, whom the law of Moses condemned to death as men or women who should not be found among God's people (Lev. 20:27).

While all this is true, we must not suppose that the wise men of Babylon practiced only evil arts. They were the learned men of the day, the astronomers who watched the movements of heavenly bodies and could predict when an eclipse would take place. Daniel and his companions had studied their science and were counted among them after they had completed their training. Of course, we would judge that the Hebrew youth would know what was legitimate practice and what was not. Furthermore, they had a source of understanding not available to their Babylonian peers.

The wise men included those called Chaldeans, members "of an Aramaean tribe whose early settlement was in lower Mesopotamia" (*The SDA Bible Commentary*, vol. 4, p. 758). Nebuchadnezzar's father had come from this tribe, and it is understandable that the king would call them in at a time of emergency. They were first to speak as they stood before the ruler with all the others ready to do his bidding.

After the introductory words of respect, "O king, live

forever," came the request: "Tell your servants the dream, and we will interpret it." They had no doubt about their ability to give an interpretation. Having long studied dreams and seen their correlation with events, they foresaw no problems in this case. All they needed to know was the dream, and the rest would be easy.

But the king was not in a position to cooperate. For some reason, which we must attribute to Providence, the dream had vanished from his mind (see *Prophets and Kings*, p. 491). "The thing is gone from me" (Dan. 2:5, KJV) was the king's reply. "I hereby decree" is the way *Tanakh: A New Translation of the Holy Scriptures According to the Traditional Hebrew Text* puts it. The NIV renders it: "This is what I have firmly decided." This other way of understanding the Aramaic text suggests that King Nebuchadnezzar may have decided that if the wise men could interpret a dream from divine sources, they could use the same sources to reveal the dream.

It is interesting to see how the wise men tried to get out of what they considered an impossible situation. On the one hand the king had offered magnificent rewards for compliance with his request or terrible calamities if they failed. On the other hand, the wise men knew their limitations and could see no escape from their dilemma. So they argued, "No one on earth can do what the king demands," "No one has ever before made such a request," "The only gods who could reveal such a matter have their abode far from human reach."

The king became furious. Was he acting as a despot, unreasonable in his demands? Or was he, perchance, recognizing a principle that if the gods they worshiped could do what they claimed to be able to do, then they would surely be able to reveal a dream that presumably they themselves had given to Nebuchadnezzar. If so, then the ruler was questioning the integrity of the gods they worshiped in Babylon. Such an element of doubt would prepare the way for the acceptance of the true God, who, as we shall see, caused the dream to be revealed.

The wise men had no doubt about his ability to carry out his threat if they failed him. Scared—and rightly so—they tried to defend their position, but the king did not accept their propositions. Nebuchadnezzar issued the decree for their annihilation, and they left the palace in abject terror.

Scripture does not explain why Daniel was not with the wise men on this occasion. To those of us who believe in the intervention of God, we can see that it was providential. It made possible the complete rout of the wise men without the prophet's immediate intervention, and it heightened the contrast between false worship and true.

Some commentators suggest that Daniel had not yet graduated from the school he attended, and so he would not have been eligible to attend. It would seem unreasonable, then, to seek him out so that he would suffer the same fate as the others. Others suggest that the counselors had not invited him since he was a captive Jew, an instance of ethnic discrimination. If the latter suggestion is true, then it brings out clearly the difference between Daniel and his Babylonian peers. They had sought to exclude him from the honor of consultation with the king, while he was anxious to do something to save their lives from destruction now that they were discredited.

Daniel learned of the decree and the reason for it when the captain of the royal guard came to pick him up for execution. No doubt shocked, he immediately asked for an interview with the king, and when brought before the ruler, he asked for time so that he might be able to comply with the king's request. Why was Nebuchadnezzar so peremptory with the wise men of Babylon and so gracious with Daniel? Scripture does not say, but we can see a difference of spirit between Daniel and his Babylonian peers. The others held out no hope of being able to meet the royal demand, while Daniel assured his king that he would come up with an answer. No doubt the king remembered that the Jewish captive had done well in his examinations. At the same time,

Daniel's confidence in being able to help the ruler in his dilemma showed the close relationship between him and his God.

The first thing Daniel did when he left Nebuchadnez-zar's presence was to summon his fellow Jews and inform them of the situation. He suggested fervent prayer that God might deliver them from death by revealing the mystery of the royal dream. And that very night a vision revealed the dream's message.

One can imagine the ecstasy of the Hebrew youth. God had come to their aid immediately. Daniel burst into poetry as he extolled the God of heaven:

"Wisdom and power are his." Wisdom to know what to do for the best, and power to do what He wants His children to do.

"He changes times and seasons." He is in full control of nature. Time is part of His creation, so that while we are subject to time, He is beyond and above it.

"He sets up kings and deposes them." The highest figure in human society, or the one who seems to have all power and can do as he pleases, is still subject to His control. That which man cannot do, God can.

"He gives wisdom to the wise and knowledge to the discerning." To those who are wise God can give more wisdom, and those who have already acquired a store of knowledge can receive even more. The intellect of man can discover much about the universe, but in the end he has to admit that with all the advances of science he has touched only the surface of what may be known.

"He reveals deep and hidden things," things that cannot be known except by revelation, and He graciously treats man as a friend and shares with him His concerns and understandings.

"He knows what lies in darkness." God's power is definitely greater than man's, for "light dwells with him."

Finally Daniel gave thanks and praise to the God of his fathers, indicating by the last phrase that he was in a succession of people who had worshiped the same God. (In the ancient world a conquoring power could replace the gods of a defeated nation with its own.) By revealing the king's dream to Daniel, He had enabled Daniel to be a truly wise man, a man who would then be able to accomplish great things for all concerned (Dan. 2:20-23).

Daniel now was able to go to the captain of the royal guard and ask him not to slay the wise men because he could supply the king with the information demanded. It is interesting to note a little human sidelight: When the officer approached Nebuchadnezzar, he said, "I have found a man!" Actually he had not *found* Daniel. But he was anxious to earn a little credit for what was to happen next!

In the introductory interview with the king, Daniel made it clear that the wise men were not in a position to interpret the dream. They were not in touch with the One who alone could convey such knowledge, the God of heaven, the God who had given the dream so that the king might know something of the future. Daniel further insisted that the mystery of the dream had not been revealed to him because he had any native intelligence greater than any other man, but in order that the king might have an answer from God regarding the questions that had been troubling him about the future. With this humble introduction Daniel proceeded to tell the king his dream, details of which must have returned to Nebuchadnezzar's consciousness as the Hebrew youth spoke.

The king had seen an image composed of various metals. The head was of gold, the arms and breast of silver, the thighs of bronze, the legs of iron, and the feet part iron, part clay. A rock cut out without human hands struck the image in the feet, and the whole image collapsed and disappeared. Meanwhile, the rock grew into a big mountain and filled the whole earth (verses 31-35).

Daniel told Nebuchadnezzar that the head of gold represented him. God had given him "dominion and power and might and glory" (verse 37). So if the Babylonian king thought it was because of his own personal achievements, he should recognize the true source of his power. Other kingdoms would follow his, but they would be inferior, just as silver and bronze were lesser in worth to gold. The iron represented a power that would be strong and crushing, but its successor would be partly strong and partly weak, just as clay is weak in relation to iron; and the two elements would never be able to blend together, just as clay and iron do not fuse.

The climax would come "in the time of those kings." That is, during the period when kingdoms would never again be able to combine into one. Then the God of heaven would set up a kingdom that would never be destroyed (verse 44).

In response, the Babylonian ruler fell prostrate before Daniel. Never before had he heard of or seen a miracle like this—that someone could make the intimacies of a dream so explicit without receiving a hint or a clue. In harmony with his pagan thinking, he ordered that an offering and incense be brought and presented to Daniel. Then he confessed, "Surely your God is the God of gods and the Lord of kings" (verse 47).

It was a day of victory for the knowledge of the true God. Nebuchadnezzar was not yet a monotheist—he still had much more to learn—but he knew that Yahweh was greater than any of the gods worshiped and honored by the Babylonians.

Living as we do some 2,500 years after his time, we can see how history has confirmed his dream in a remarkable way. The empire of the Medes and Persians succeeded the Neo-Babylonian empire, and in turn came Greece and Rome. Rome was certainly a powerful political structure that ruthlessly crushed all opposition. And then followed a divided Europe unable to unite in spite of many attempts, some nations being strong and others weak. Now we await the setting up of God's eternal kingdom that nothing will ever destroy.

The second chapter of Daniel ends with the prophet being made ruler over the entire province of Babylon. His companions also received positions of high rank. It must have been a time of great rejoicing for God's people everywhere. God had once again vindicated His name, and we see without a doubt that He is in control of what happens on earth. History leads to one goal—the establishment of God's eternal kingdom. As certainly as prophecy has been fulfilled, so certainly will God's kingdom be set up. It is now for everyone to bow before the God of the universe, accept His sovereignty, and band every energy to the accomplishment of His purposes.

PRINCIPLES OF LIFE

Here are some more propositions for you to consider:

1. It is foolish for us to suppose that we can lay plans for our lives and execute them without recognizing that there is a God whose sovereignty we must take into account.

2. The future is not threatening to one who realizes that God is in control.

3. When it comes to knowing the future, only One can unlock it with certainty. To turn to crystal-ball gazing or palm reading or any other such method in the search for future events is foolish.

4. God reveals the future, not to satisfy curiosity, but to indicate that He is the one true God and to help us be prepared to deal with coming events.

5. Prayer—group prayer—is Heaven's ordained means of finding solutions to our problems.

6. The man of God is as much interested in the welfare of others as he is in his own.

7. If we are wise, we shall acknowledge divine sovereignty in every area of our lives.

8. God employs human agents to accomplish His purposes.

9. It is a great privilege to be an instrument that God can use for bringing good to others.

WORTH NOTING:

"The strength of nations, as of individuals, is not found in the opportunities or facilities that appear to make them invincible; it is not found in their boasted greatness. It is measured by the fidelity with which they fulfill God's purpose" *(Prophets and Kings*, p. 502).

"In His law God has made known the principles that underlie all true prosperity, both of nations and of individuals. To the Israelites Moses declared of this law: 'This is your wisdom and your understanding.' 'It is not a vain thing for you; because it is your life.' Deuteronomy 4:6; 32:47. The blessings thus assured to Israel are, on the same conditions and in the same degree, assured to every nation and to every individual under the broad heavens" *(ibid.*, pp. 500, 501).

A Lesson
From History:
Our God Is Able

"We have nothing to fear for the future, except as we shall forget the way the Lord has led us, and His teaching in our past history" (Life Sketches, p. 196).

Having read in chapter 2 how Nebuchadnezzar came to recognize the God of heaven, we are disappointed to learn in chapter 3 that the king had apparently reverted to paganism. How did this happen?

Commentators have made a number of suggestions:

1. The Babylonian counselors, although they owed their lives to Daniel, became jealous of his rise to administrative power and began to undermine his influence. They pointed out that he was not a Babylonian but basically a foreign captive, and he might one day become a traitor.

2. Playing on Nebuchadnezzar's pride of achievement, they suggested that his kingdom of gold could never pass away. They proposed that the king should set up an image like the one he had seen in his dream so that all could see it and admire the head of gold.

3. The king went a little further by commanding that the image be all of gold. The trouble was that Nebuchadnezzar and his advisers had forgotten three important things:

    a. They had forgotten the providential circumstances connected with the dream and its interpretation;

    b. They had forgotten that they owed their lives to the fact that Daniel had explained the dream;

c. They forgot everything except their one desire to make themselves and their empire as great as possible. But to do so, they had to set aside the concept of God's hand in history and make man the arbiter of his own destiny.

Thus Nebuchadnezzar reverted to his idol worship "with increased zeal and bigotry" (see *Prophets and Kings,* pp. 504, 505).

We can understand how the pressure on him must have been great. A cuneiform tablet informs us that Babylon contained 53 temples dedicated to important gods, 955 small sanctuaries, and 384 street altars (see *The SDA Bible Commentary,* vol. 4, p. 797). Babylon was a center of religious activity greater than any other ancient city. The center of the city contained a temple complex that "was the largest and most famous of all the temples of the ancient Orient" (*ibid.,* p. 798). "In this temple stood the statue of Marduk, from which the king received his royalty each year when he 'took the hand of Marduk' at the New Year Festival" (McKenzie, "Babylon," *Dictionary of the Bible).* Marduk was the head of the pantheon of gods, and the Epic of Creation recounts his exploits (cf. A. Heidel, *The Babylonian Genesis).* It would not be easy for Nebuchadnezzar to accept the biblical account of Creation when his own culture and literature viewed things from so different a perspective. Thus the king yielded to the pressures around him and set up an image on the plain of Dura.

Daniel does not tell us in which year of the king's reign this event took place. But the years after the dream were ones of great activity. The struggle with Egypt in 601 B.C. proved disappointing to Nebuchadnezzar. After a year of rest in Babylon came a campaign in northwest Arabia in which his forces seized much plunder from the desert Arabs. The following year saw Jerusalem besieged and then taken on March 16, 597 B.C. The Babylonian forces took Jehoiachin, king of Judah, captive to Babylon and put Zedekiah in his place. Jeremiah tells us that Zedekiah went to Babylon in the fourth year of his reign (594/593 B.C.). Some have suggested it might have been the year that Nebuchadnezzar erected his image. Zedekiah would have gone because of the summons we read about in Daniel 3:2.

If that was the case, then two kings of Judah would have been present at the site of the image besides the Hebrew youths. It makes the courage of the young men to refuse to bow down even more outstanding. Furthermore, Jeremiah had prepared a scroll that was to be taken to Babylon at this time and read. (It is recorded in Jeremiah 51:1-58.) Jeremiah's messenger was to read the scroll and then tie a stone to it and throw it into the Euphrates, saying, "So will Babylon sink to rise no more because of the disaster I will bring upon her. And her people will fall" (verse 64). It is interesting to note that at the same time Babylon proclaimed its greatness, God announced its fall.

Daniel gives us a vivid picture of the scene at Dura. The image of gold, 90 feet high, gleamed in the sun. Somewhere nearby, the furnace, ominously blazing, waited to devour whoever might dare to disobey the king's command. The crowd of people, all dressed in their robes of office, stood expectantly for the signal to be given. An orchestra with a great variety of musical instruments waited to play. The king's herald loudly gave instructions on what to do. And Nebuchadnezzar himself, surrounded by his bodyguard, gazed on the multitude and glanced up to the image with great pride. At a signal a sea of heads bowed down before the image. But three young men remained upright.

Normally they would not have been seen, but some of the wise men of Babylon had their eyes open. They knew where they might expect refusal to give homage to an image. And they saw what they were hoping to see, because now they could make a damning accusation before the king. Nor were they slow to do so.

It is interesting to note the stings of their report. The recalcitrants were Jews—bad enough! The king had placed them in high governmental positions—obviously a mistake!

They paid no attention to his command—how ungrateful and discourteous! And they refused to serve the king's gods or worship the image—an affront of a most serious nature! Not surprisingly, the king was furious. He was human and he expected to be obeyed. It was his moment of glory, and he was unwilling to brook dissent. Angrily he called for the three young men by name—Shadrach, Meshach, and Abednego. Obviously he knew them and their background. Giving them an opportunity to confess their guilt, he asked, "Is it true?" Extending to them a second chance, he warned them of the blazing furnace. Finally he asked the crucial question, "What god will be able to rescue you from my hand?" (Dan. 3:15).

The whole ceremony came to a halt. A furious king, shaking from head to toe, faced three young men who stood remarkably calm. The accusers stood by, watching the confrontation with glee, expecting victory. The multitude questioned among itself as to what had happened. The soldiers remained at attention, waiting for orders.

The three young men spoke with confidence and reason. "We do not need to defend ourselves before you in this matter" (verse 16). In many private sessions they had already explained to the king their allegiance to Yahweh, the God of their fathers. He knew that they could not in good conscience bow down before any idol, for it would violate one of the commandments of the Decalogue given to Moses on tablets of stone. As for the blazing furnace—and here they gave an amazing testimony—"the God we serve is able to save us from it, and he will rescue us from your hand, O king" (verse 17).

There was, of course, the possibility that God would not see fit to rescue them, would not save them from the blazing furnace. Man does not control God. He does not make God do anything he wants, whether by faith or prayer or anything else. Prayer and faith have their place in the Christian experience, but God is always free to do as He sees best, and we would not have it otherwise. Hence the three

young men added, "But even if he does not, we want you to
know, O king, that we will not serve your gods or worship the
image of gold you have set up" (verse 19). Their worship of
God was absolute, without any strings attached. Here was
faith of the highest order, allegiance that was exemplary.

Once again Nebuchadnezzar flew into a rage. No longer
would he try to save them; instead he ordered the furnace to
be heated up even further, supposing thereby to make the
possibility of escape so much more remote. Then he had the
victims bound by the strongest soldiers and thrown into the
furnace. The tragedy was that the guards perished from the
intensity of the heat without the flames even touching them.
But there was no doubt that the three young men had fallen
into the midst of the blaze.

All eyes now centered on this new development.
Attention focused not on the image but on the furnace.
Assuming that King Jehoiachin and King Zedekiah were
there with all their retinue, can one imagine the thoughts
that must have raced through their minds? Is there a time
when compromise is acceptable? Is it permissible to
dissemble a little to save one's life? Such questions
doubtless come to us in moments of crisis, and they are
ones that we must settle beforehand. Only then can we take
the kind of stand that the three young men did. Are we
making now the preparations necessary for us to be ready to
meet any emergency? The stories we read in the Bible
encourage us to prepare for crises *before* they arrive.

Excitement surged through the crowd as in amazement
Nebuchadnezzar leaped to his feet. Four men now walked
around in the fire, and he could not understand it. One of
them looked like "a son of the gods" (verse 25). (This is a
literal translation from the Aramaic. Even in the Hebrew the
word for God is in a plural form, so the KJV is correct in
translating the phrase as "the Son of God.")

"How did that heathen king know what the Son of God
was like? The Hebrew captives filling positions of trust in
Babylon had in life and character represented before him

LDS-4

the truth. When asked for a reason for their faith, they had given it without hesitation. Plainly and simply they had presented the principles of righteousness, thus teaching those around them of the God whom they worshiped. They had told of Christ, the Redeemer to come; and in the form of the fourth in the midst of the fire the king recognized the Son of God" *(Prophets and Kings,* p. 509).

On two other occasions the preincarnate Christ appeared in fire—the burning bush that Moses saw (Ex. 3) and the Angel Manoah saw ascending in flame (Judges 13:20).

Nebuchadnezzar called the three young men "servants of the Most High God." Once again the king recognized the God above all gods. It speaks well for him that he did not deny the evidence before him. He may not have been a monotheist yet, but at least he recognized an authority higher than any of the deities he had worshiped before.

The whole assembled mass of people witnessed the miracle. They saw that the fire had not burned any part of their bodies or clothing. Not even the smell of smoke lingered on them. What a testimony they would take back to their territories. Instead of the greatness of the king of Babylon, they would talk of the majesty of the God of heaven. The three young men would long be the target of questions as people sought to understand what had happened that day and why. Even among the captives of Judah—those who knew the Scriptures well—many would want to hear for themselves the testimony of the three young men. Once again, through three fearless and uncompromising youth, God's name had been vindicated.

Nebuchadnezzar's response to the situation was one that we might expect from a pagan king used to exercising power. He not only praised the God of Shadrach, Meshach, and Abednego, he issued a decree that anyone of any nation or language who spoke against Him would be hacked to pieces and his house demolished. In praising God he was well within his rights, but in seeking to compel compliance to a religious faith he exceeded his rights as a temporal ruler. The Arabs say it well: "There is no compulsion in religion." Not even God forces obedience to His law. Man is free to choose whom he will serve, but when he has made his choice, he alone is responsible for his actions.

What about us and the future? "As in the days of Shadrach, Meshach, and Abednego, so in the closing period of earth's history the Lord will work mightily in behalf of those who stand steadfastly for the right. He who walked with the Hebrew worthies in the fiery furnace will be with His followers wherever they are. His abiding presence will comfort and sustain" *(Prophets and Kings,* p. 513).

We have no reason to fear the future or any of its contingencies so long as we determine to do what is right and God is by our side.

PRINCIPLES OF LIFE

1. It is easy to revert to wicked ways, even after conversion, unless one maintains a close connection with the Bible and the church.

2. It is safer to be criticized than to be praised.

3. We must always guard against flattery.

4. Death with honor is preferable to spiritual compromise and continued life.

5. The decision to do right is always a personal decision.

6. The one who determines to do right, regardless of the consequences, is never alone; God is by his side.

7. It is always dangerous to do what everyone else is doing simply because everyone does it.

Now add some of your own:

8.

9.

10.

WORTH NOTING:

"On that eventful day the powers of darkness seemed to be gaining a signal triumph; the worship of the golden image bade fair to become connected permanently with the established forms of idolatry recognized as the state religion of the land. Satan hoped thereby to defeat God's purpose of making the presence of captive Israel in Babylon a means of blessing to all the nations of heathendom" *(Prophets and Kings*, p. 506).

"Important are the lessons to be learned from the experience of the Hebrew youth on the plain of Dura. In this our day, many of God's servants, though innocent of wrongdoing, will be given over to suffer humiliation and abuse at the hands of those who, inspired by Satan, are filled with envy and religious bigotry. Especially will the wrath of man be aroused against those who hallow the Sabbath of the fourth commandment; and at last a universal decree will denounce these as deserving of death" *(ibid.*, p. 512).

A King Is Humbled:
The Measure
of True Greatness

"Nebuchadnezzar had learned at last the lesson which all rulers need to learn—that true greatness consists in true goodness" (Prophets and Kings, p. 521).

The fourth chapter of the book of Daniel differs significantly from the other chapters in the book. The author is Nebuchadnezzar himself rather than Daniel, although the prophet may have had a hand in its composition. The style is that of a formal letter in which the author begins by announcing his name, indicates the ones to whom he has written, and then expresses a greeting. The terminology of praise reminds one of Psalm 143, which does not fit in with the king's cultural background, but may reflect the help that Daniel provided as the king sought suitable language to express himself.

The king addresses everyone, apparently feeling that his testimony should go to every person in the world, whatever the race, the nation, or the language. He wishes everyone great prosperity and says that it is his pleasure to testify to the miracles and wonders that the Most High has performed on his behalf. As he speaks of God's miracles and wonders and the fact that His kingdom is an everlasting one that "endures from generation to generation" (Dan. 4:3), he waxes into poetry.

The king then goes on to relate how he was in his palace, "contented and prosperous," when he had a dream that frightened him. In fact, as he thought of the details of the dream, it terrified him. So he summoned the wise men of Babylon to the palace to interpret the dream, and when they arrived—magicians, enchanters, astrologers, and diviners—he recounted his dream, but they could not interpret it.

It reminds us of a former occasion when the king had a dream and the professional diviners could not help him. Of course, the situation was different at that time in the sense that the king had been unwilling or unable to recall the dream. This time he remembered and recounted it. Why were the professional interpreters of dreams unable to explain its significance?

It may have been that they recognized the dream as an ill omen, and they did not want to convey bad news to the king. If so, they should have said so. Their confession that they were unable to interpret the dream must have once more confirmed Nebuchadnezzar's doubts regarding the validity of the profession as a whole. In any case, Daniel enters the room where the king holds his audiences, and the king proceeds to tell him the dream.

In a little aside Nebuchadnezzar identifies Daniel as Belteshazzar, named after the king's god. There seems to be a hint here that the Babylonian ruler has a special regard for this Hebrew captive who had been so helpful to him in the past. He also affirms that in Daniel is the "spirit of the holy gods," a phrase certainly in harmony with his polytheistic culture. But he is in his own way giving Daniel the highest compliment that anyone can give. It is more than a compliment of genius or learning—it recognizes the close contact between the man and his God, his noble character, and his wise counsel.

The dream seems simple enough in its outline. The king saw a large tree whose top reached toward the sky. Visible from everywhere, it produced abundant fruit, providing food for all. Birds lived among the branches, and animals took shelter in its shade. What was frightening was the appearance of a messenger, a holy one from heaven, who with a loud voice gave orders to hew down the tree and cut off its branches. No longer would it offer fruit and shelter to animals and birds. Only the stump was to remain in the ground, "bound with iron and bronze."

The language of the holy messenger then changes to suggest that the tree represents a person who will be drenched with the dew of heaven. His mind will change from that of a man to that of an animal, and "seven times" will pass over him. But all this will happen to prove to all living that "the Most High is sovereign over the kingdoms of men."

The king appeals to Daniel to interpret the dream because the wise men of Babylon were not able to do so. "But you can," he says, "because the spirit of the holy gods is in you" (verse 18).

For a time Daniel is greatly perplexed. He can see the dream does not bode well for the king and is not sure whether the ruler will accept its message. But Nebuchadnezzar encourages him to go ahead. Most likely the king already had a good idea of its general meaning.

Daniel points out his wish that the dream should befall Nebuchadnezzar's enemies rather than him. But the fact is that the tree represents the king in his greatness as ruler of Babylon. His influence reaches out to the distant parts of the earth. But the Most High has determined that the time had come when the king would have to lose his royal position. He would become like an animal for seven years, but when he acknowledged that the Most High is sovereign over the earth, able to do what He pleases, then he would return to his senses, and God would restore the kingdom to him.

Immediately Daniel hastens to advise the king to renounce his sins, to do what is right, to be kind to the oppressed, and then it may happen that he will avoid the calamity.

The dream is indeed fulfilled. Twelve months later, as the king walks on the flat roof of his palace, he admires the wonderful buildings that he has been instrumental in constructing. "Is not this the great Babylon I have built?" he says to himself (verses 29, 30). Immediately a voice comes from heaven pronouncing sentence. Removed from human society, the king acts like an animal. He eats grass like cattle. His hair grows like feathers, and his nails begin to resemble the claws of a bird. But at the end of the seven-year period Nebuchadnezzar gazes toward heaven and acknowledges the sovereignty and greatness of God. At that very time his sanity returns, and he regains his kingdom.

The whole episode must have been embarrassing for the king to relate. But the fact that he describes it in such detail indicates a sincere conversion. He had no doubt in his mind as to who was in control in the world. God is the one who blesses with life and health. He calls men and women to accomplish His purposes, and He alone determines the beginning and the end. The sooner we recognize that all that we are or hope to be depends on God, the sooner we shall be able to lead lives of usefulness and praise. It is God who created us in His image, and it is through His goodness and grace that we can reflect that image. If we do not reflect such an image, our lives are no better than that of animals.

"The once proud monarch had become a humble child of God; the tyrannical, overbearing ruler, a wise and compassionate king. He who had defied and blasphemed the God of heaven now acknowledged the power of the Most High and earnestly sought to promote the fear of Jehovah and the happiness of his subjects" (*Prophets and Kings*, p. 521).

PRINCIPLES OF LIFE

Would you agree with the following propositions?

1. We can hide our true selves from many people, but we cannot hide from God. We are to Him as an open book.

2. Happy is the man who recognizes his dependence upon God and is willing to confess it.

3. When we acknowledge our weaknesses, we do not lose influence with our fellowmen, but gain it.

4. Greatness is not standing above our fellows and ordering them around—it is standing with them and helping them to be all that they can be.

5. Those who are truly great are those who are truly good.

Now add a few propositions of your own:

6.

7.

8.

WORTH NOTING:

"Only those who love and fear God can understand the mysteries of the kingdom of heaven" (*Prophets and Kings*, p. 516).

"The heart that is not transformed by the grace of God soon loses the impressions of the Holy Spirit" (*ibid.*, p. 519).

Handwriting on the Wall: Consequences of Persistent Wrongdoing

"The history of nations speaks to us today. To every nation and to every individual God has assigned a place in His great plan. Today men and nations are being tested by the plummet in the hand of Him who makes no mistake. All are by their own choice deciding their destiny, and God is overruling all for the accomplishment of His purposes" (Prophets and Kings, p. 536).

The fifth chapter of Daniel relates an incident that has become so well known, in fact, that the phrase "see the handwriting on the wall" (meaning to recognize the signs of impending disaster or misfortune) has become a firm part of the English language.

The last two verses of Daniel 5 tell us when the incident took place; it was the fateful last night of the Neo-Babylonian empire, the time when the Medo-Persian forces would take over the reins of government. Historians give us the date of October 12, 539 B.C.

How long was this after Nebuchadnezzar's dream, recorded in the previous chapter? Historians tell us it may have been about 33 years. Nebuchadnezzar died in 562 B.C. His son, Amel-Marduk, called Evil-Merodach in the Bible (2 Kings 25:27; Jer. 52:31), ascended the throne and, perhaps remembering his father's appreciation of Daniel's interpretation of dreams, showed favor to Jehoiachin, king of Judah, and released him from prison. He gave him a seat of honor above other hostage kings in Babylon and provided him with rations from the royal palace for the rest of his life. Unfortunately, Amel-Marduk did not reign long, for after two years his brother-in-law Neriglissar killed him and ruled in his stead. Neriglissar governed for four years, and although after his death his son received the throne as king, a Babylonian noble called Nabu-Naid (Nabonidus), with the help of some courtiers, did away with him and seized the position for himself.

It seems that Nabonidus, being the son of a priestess of the Temple of the Moon in Haran, was a devotee of the moon god, Sin. When he tried to change Babylonian religious life, he met with resistance, became unpopular, and decided that he would entrust the kingship to his eldest son in Babylon, while he occupied himself with other matters. After campaigning in Syria and northern Arabia, Nabonidus spent about 10 years in Tema, assuming the rulership there.

One can see that with all this going on, the Neo-Babylonian empire was weakening rapidly. With trusted servants the wheels of government still turned, but with rapid changes in leadership, and no one providing any dynamic direction, the empire was divided and helpless before the attack. One wonders what Daniel might have thought of all this. He does not tell us, but we may be sure that he had not forgotten Nebuchadnezzar's first dream and was watching with great interest to see how prophecy would be fulfilled.

Belshazzar

Belshazzar was Nabonidus' eldest son, the one entrusted with kingship in Babylon. He began his coregency with his father about 553 B.C., suggesting that he had reigned for about 13 years by the time of the incident in chapter five. Daniel would be in his eighties, still capable of holding office, but apparently not active in government at this time. It is highly probable that Belshazzar never felt comfortable with Daniel, concluding that he had no need of advice from the one who had been so close to Nebuchadnezzar. We shall soon see why he would react that way.

The Great Feast

It was not unusual for kings to have magnificent feasts in ancient times. We read of one in Esther 1:3-12. But a banquet at this time in Babylon showed extremely poor taste. Sippar, a town only a few miles to the north, had already fallen into the hands of the invading Median forces. Yet Belshazzar apparently felt perfectly safe within the protective walls of Babylon. If he felt any fears, perhaps he thought he could drown them in drinking and orgy. Regardless, his banquet at this time suggests irresponsibility.

The fact that he could call upon a thousand of the nobles and princes of Babylon to join him in the feasting indicates that many shared his unconcern. The times really called for serious planning and preparation, not for carousing. But Belshazzar and his companions had no such thoughts in mind.

Perhaps having the feast was a form of bravado, of whistling in the dark to keep one's courage up in time of danger. In any case it was not the kind of activity that any sober person would engage in at a time of peril. In view of the situation, we are not really surprised at the outcome.

What really amazes the reader is that the king had the audacity to order the sacred vessels of the Temple at Jerusalem brought into the feast to be used as part of the drunken revelry. Even as a pagan king, he should have had more respect than that. Nebuchadnezzar had placed them in the temples of his gods, treating them with respect as more than common objects.

Even though Jerusalem was a conquered city and its inhabitants had been taken captive, honorable people would recognize that religious objects and places of worship should receive respect. We may not agree with others in their forms of worship, we may not share their religious teachings, but we must always respect their religious convictions. Any form of desecration is horrifying. To drink from vessels dedicated to religious purposes is bad enough, but to follow it up with praise of other gods added insult to injury.

God's Response to the Situation

"In the same hour." The response came without delay. In some instances God can be gracious and forgiving. He can delay action until people realize what they are doing. But sometimes nothing is gained by waiting. God can see that those performing the evil are perfectly aware of what they are doing, and they do so with careful thought and deliberation. If the act involves any insult, they recognize it and proceed anyway. In such instances God's response needs to be immediate. Belshazzar and his feast represented a willful and deliberate case of blasphemy.

Suddenly the king observed a hand with fingers writing on the plastered wall opposite his throne. Recognizing that a Being of great authority was addressing him, he felt great fear seize him, a fear that left his body trembling uncontrollably. His thoughts raced and his spirits plummeted. Face contorted in agony, he shouted for someone to bring in the wise men of the land in order to explain the strange writing to him.

One can understand the confusion that must have developed as everyone sought to discover what was the matter. After what seemed an eternity, the wise men arrived one by one as located. In his haste the king made an immediate promise that if anyone could read and interpret the inscription, the king would clothe him with scarlet, place a chain of gold about his neck, and appoint him third ruler in the kingdom. Soon all the wise men were present, but none of them could solve the mystery.

We can imagine the silence as the wise men concentrated on their task. The king and his nobles stared into their faces, seeking some inkling of understanding. The anxiety of the king increased until he finally writhed in agony while the lords stood around with their wives and concubines, feeling absolutely helpless. What of the merrymaking now?

It had burst like a bubble. Where was the sense of security and safety? It had vanished into thin air. And now there was a sense of imminent danger, of misfortune about to fall on them.

The Queen Mother Comes In

Word of the consternation and confusion in the banqueting hall soon spread throughout the palace. News reached the chambers of the queen mother, who hurried to see what she could do. Concerned about her son and his safety, she wanted to restore some kind of order. As a woman of experience, held in high regard, she felt sure that she could help in the emergency.

By entering the banqueting hall unsummoned, she had broken the rules of court etiquette, but no one at the moment was concerned about protocol. She observed that the writing on the wall had completely baffled the wise men, and she remembered other occasions when this had happened. Nebuchadnezzar, she recalled, had called the court counselors on at least two occasions and they had not been able to solve the mystery.

But one man had succeeded when others had failed. His name was Daniel, a former president of the association of wise men, but now retired. Retired not because he could no longer function, but because his ideas of the source of true wisdom were no longer popular. In him resided the spirit of the holy gods, an expression that conveyed the high regard of those who knew and loved him, though they did not necessarily agree with his philosophy of life.

Quickly the queen mother approached the dais where the king sat, and tried to comfort him. With proper respect she addressed him, "O king, live forever." Then she told him not to worry because she knew of someone who could solve the mystery of the supernatural writing. "Let him be called" was the reply.

Probably Belshazzar would not likely be interested in someone like Daniel, who had so impressed his grandfather with his devotion to God. Apparently the current Babylonian ruler did not want to have anything to do with it; he had pursued his own way of life with total disregard of such former wise men as Daniel. But now the situation was urgent, so he swallowed his pride. "Let Daniel be called. Let Daniel speak."

In due course—after what seemed to be a period of intolerable agony—servants ushered Daniel into the king's presence. He walked with measured dignity. Swift glances around him apprised him of the situation. Though not really surprised, he was disgusted. It was obvious that God, in a remarkable way, had brought the drunken orgy to an end. Courteously he waited for the king's command.

The king grudgingly recognized Daniel with a barbed comment. He claimed to remember him as one of the captives of Judah, one whom his predecessor had brought from Jerusalem. However, he had to admit that he had also heard of him as one in whom was the "spirit of the gods." Did Daniel notice that he had left out the word holy? Obviously this was not a characteristic that interested Belshazzar. But he did recognize wisdom. As he described the predicament of the wise men in not being able to read and interpret the inscription on the wall, he paid Daniel a reluctant compliment: "I have heard that you are able to give interpretations and to solve difficult problems" (Dan. 5:16). Yet quickly he added, "If you can read this writing . . ." Apparently he was not convinced of the old man's talent, but he did repeat the rewards he had offered before to the wise men.

The prophet brushed aside the introductory speech and turned down what would seem to have been a magnificent offer. But he would interpret the writing for the king.

What follows next is both a lesson of history and a stinging rebuke. The history lesson reminded Belshazzar what God—the Most High God—had done for his predecessor, Nebuchadnezzar. The Lord had given him power to do as he pleased, and then humbled him when he became arrogant and disregarded the source of his power. The rebuke was that Belshazzar knew all this but had not learned the lesson. He had set himself up "against the Lord of heaven" (verse 23) by misusing the sacred vessels of the Temple at Jerusalem. Hence the writing on the wall.

The message was brief but ominous. God had decided that the reign of Belshazzar had come to an end. The Babylonian ruler had been weighed in the balances of truth and found wanting, lacking in the qualities that make for leadership. The kingdom was to be divided, taken away from him, and given to the Medes and the Persians. Three words of doom: *Mene, Tekel, Peres.*

One wonders how Belshazzar felt at the time. Was he too drunk to grasp the significance of the revelation? Somehow he gave orders that Daniel be honored as he had been promised. But it all meant nothing, because the king perished that night and a new empire assumed power.

PRINCIPLES OF LIFE

The following propositions seem to come out of a study of the fifth chapter of the book of Daniel. Do you agree with them?

1. Rulers have a solemn obligation to learn the lessons of history.

2. All who have positions of responsibility affecting the lives of others must do what is right and not just that which pleases them.

3. God lets a person do what he wants to do, but that person must be prepared to reap the consequences.

4. God does not leave anyone ignorant of His requirements. He has messengers always available at the time of need.

5. We must not forget our dependence upon God for everything.

WORTH NOTING:

"The present is a time of overwhelming interest to all living. Rulers and statesmen, men who occupy positions of trust and authority, thinking men and women of all classes, have their attention fixed upon the events taking place about us. They are watching the relations that exist among the nations. They observe the intensity that is taking possession of every earthly element, and they recognize that something great and decisive is about to take place—that the world is on the verge of a stupendous crisis.

"The Bible, and the Bible only, gives a correct view of these things. Here are revealed the great final scenes in the history of our world, events that are already casting their shadows before, the sound of their approach causing the earth to tremble and men's hearts to fail them for fear" (*Prophets and Kings*, p. 537).

A Den of Lions: Safety in Rightdoing

"A man whose heart is stayed upon God will be the same in the hour of his greatest trial as he is in prosperity, when the light and favor of God and of man beam upon him. Faith reaches to the unseen, and grasps eternal realities" (Prophets and Kings, p. 545).

God has not promised us a bed of roses in the present life. Although the Christian life has many blessings, we also often face moments of great trial. We meet with unnecessary opposition from those who claim to love us. Suffering injustice, we wonder why God permits it. Sickness or accident strikes us or our loved ones. Sometimes doing the right thing seems to invite disaster or even death. What are we to do?

We all know that we should always do the right thing. But when that leads to losing our position, the work that means so much to us and to our families, does God expect us to make impossible sacrifices? Does He expect us to throw away our life and opportunities? Only one who has been in such a predicament understands the mental anguish that can go with making such a decision.

Perhaps the ultimate question is one of faith and trust. Can we trust God to provide for us when apparently there is so much that we need to do for ourselves? It is not so much a matter of can He as of will He? We all recognize that God can—but do we recognize that He will?

When such questions arise, we can turn to the Bible to

see how God has acted in the past. In the sixth chapter of the book of Daniel we read about how a man of God made a decision in the face of trying circumstances and how God rewarded him.

The year is 539 B.C., and the Neo-Babylonian empire has come to an ignoble end. A 62-year-old stranger called Darius the Mede has taken over the reigns of government. All those who hold positions in government wonder what will happen to them. Usually in such circumstances, those occupying positions of trust in the previous government find themselves pushed aside. They lobby endlessly, frantically, for favor. Every man for himself now!

Can we sit back and let God work out what is best for us? Some would say yes and assure us that that was exactly what happened in their case. Others would say that God helps those who help themselves. We cannot expect God to do for us what He expects us to do for ourselves. Is there a middle road between the two extremes? If so, what is it?

In the case of Daniel, we read that Darius entered upon a new administrative plan, and he chose Daniel to be one of the top three administrators. Then we read, "Now Daniel so distinguished himself among the administrators and the satraps by his exceptional qualities that the king planned to set him over the whole kingdom" (Dan. 6:3). Daniel had certain talents that God had given him. By divine grace he used them to the best of his ability. The result was the possibility of promotion.

In these few words we have the secret of success. God gives the potential; we put forth the effort that it takes to develop our skills and then use them unselfishly for the benefit of the employer, always recognizing that it is God who gives us the life, health, strength, and opportunities and that we are to cooperate with His plan for us.

But doing that does not automatically make life easy. We will always encounter those who, jealous of our position or success, would like to bring about our downfall. Daniel had his fellow administrators. But they did not have an easy time finding a case against him. He was never corrupt, never negligent, but always trustworthy (verse 4). So they turned to some phase of his religious life, feeling sure that he would never change his religious practices for any man-made law—and they were right!

The other administrators worked behind Daniel's back. How often we find the same kind of behavior in our own experience, and it annoys us! We never feel so much like fighting as we do in such situations. In time we begin to lose confidence in all our fellowmen. Although we hope that heads of administration will be astute enough not to be deceived, only too frequently they are, and we are the ones to suffer. Unless we have that kind of confidence in God that Daniel apparently had, we will feel utterly helpless.

"In God I trust; I will not be afraid. What can mortal man do to me?" said the psalmist (Ps. 56:4). Or again, "The Lord is with me; I will not be afraid. What can man do to me?" (Ps. 118:6).

In order to impress the king the administrators visited him in force. As a group they felt stronger. Then they claimed to have all agreed on their proposed ordinance (verse 7). Actually they had not, because they had not consulted Daniel. But a little lie did not matter so long as they got their way! How very human these people were! And men have not changed much since.

The appeal to the king involved his ego. No one should offer any prayer to any god except to him for a period of 30 days. It seemed a perfectly harmless decree, because anyone who wanted to pray to a god could surely postpone his petition for a month. To some, such a decree seemed not only harmless but even useless. Of course, it might bring some benefit to the king if he wished to make a charge. But the king was not astute enough to see through the plans of his administrators, and he approved the signing of the decree.

The scheme to entrap Daniel worked perfectly, for he did not hesitate to go to his room and pray three times a day as was his custom. His windows were open toward Jerusalem, so there was no difficulty monitoring his actions. Delighted, the administrators reported their findings to the king. Tradition held that the laws of the Medes and Persians could not be annulled and had to be enforced. Therefore the king would have to have Daniel thrown to the lions, and then the administrators would be free from a colleague whose standards were so high that they had no room for a little "innocent" corruption.

The king now knew that he had been caught in a trap. He wanted to get out of executing the law because he had a high regard for Daniel, but his administrators would not let him. They accused Daniel of being an exiled Jew who had no regard for the royal wishes. Actually, the old prophet probably had more respect for the king's legitimate desires than the administrators had. Loyal to his ruler, he would protect royal interests but would do so fairly and properly with everyone. Daniel had no favorites, would accept no bribes. Such uprightness was foreign to most bureaucrats. For this reason Daniel's colleagues sought to eliminate him.

Scripture declares that the king worked until sundown to try to save Daniel's life. But his efforts were in vain. It was a case in which right was on his side, but not the law. How often the innocent suffer because of legal technicalities! And how often the guilty get released because of them. Too often lawyers are more concerned with winning cases or defending their clients rather than seeing that justice is done.

So guards seized Daniel and hurled him into the lions' den. Although his colleagues rejoiced, the king was sad, telling him, "May your God, whom you serve continually, rescue you!" (verse 16). At such times, words seem quite inadequate. We must honor the Persian ruler for his concern, but most people would despise him for his weakness.

How did Daniel feel? Scripture does not say, but he would not be human if he did not have some element of fear.

He could not be sure that God would rescue him. While he knew that ultimately God would save him, that did not mean he might not suffer death, perhaps as food for lions. But we can also share the joy that must have come to him when he realized that God had closed the mouths of the beasts. Did they snuggle close to him like big cats and keep him warm? Could he sleep that night, or was his mind occupied with countless questions and problems? We do not know. One thing is sure: he was awake to respond to the king's urgent question in the morning regarding his safety.

PRINCIPLES OF LIFE

The following propositions seem to arise out of a study of the sixth chapter of Daniel. Do you agree with them as legitimate conclusions?

1. Yielding to flattery only leads to trouble.

2. Success in life depends on the diligent use of God-given talents and being faithful wherever God has placed us.

3. What a man does to hurt someone else will very likely boomerang back on him.

4. If God be for us, who can do any real harm to us?

5. Daniel was blameless, but it was not his innocence that saved him; it was God.

6. Human laws may well be concerned with human relationships, but they must not presume to regulate man's relationship with God.

7. Anyone dedicated to God and enjoying success will likely have worldly-minded people jealous of him.

WORTH NOTING:

"He [Daniel] was an example of what every businessman may become when his heart is converted and consecrated, and when his motives are right in the sight of God" *(Prophets and Kings*, p. 546).

"From the story of Daniel's deliverance we may learn that in seasons of trial and gloom God's children should be just what they were when their prospects were bright with hope and their surroundings all that they could desire. . . . A man whose heart is stayed upon God will be the same in the hour of his greatest trial as he is in prosperity" *(ibid.,* p. 545).

"God did not prevent Daniel's enemies from casting him into the lions' den; He permitted evil angels and wicked men thus far to accomplish their purpose; but it was that He might make the deliverance of His servant more marked, and the defeat of the enemies of truth and righteousness more complete" *(ibid.,* pp. 543, 544).

"Thus the prophet boldly yet quietly and humbly declared that no earthly power has a right to interpose between the soul and God. . . . Daniel stands before the world today a worthy example of Christian fearlessness and fidelity" *(ibid.,* p. 542).

"Daniel concluded that the maintenance of his testimony was more important than the continuance of his life" (Leon J. Wood, p. 82).

"Too often Christians are reluctant to witness to people in high positions, but this should not be" *(ibid.,* p. 84).

FOR FURTHER THOUGHT AND DISCUSSION

1. Should Daniel have closed his windows and prayed in secret in order to avoid being accused of breaking the law?

2. What was so unusual about his holding a high position in the administration of Darius the Mede?

3. Was he pleased when those who had plotted against him were thrown to the lions?

4. Is it good to have laws, like those of the Medes and the Persians, that are always strictly enforced?

Worldly Powers and a Heavenly Court

"Now all has been heard; here is the conclusion of the matter: Fear God and keep his commandments, for this is the whole duty of man. For God will bring every deed into judgment, including every hidden thing, whether it is good or evil" (Eccl. 12:13, 14).

Introduction

With the seventh chapter Daniel begins the second half of his book. In the first half he told us about himself and his three companions and their varied experiences while in exile. They had decided to maintain their identity as people of God while at the same time performing their duties to the best of their ability. In doing so, they had saved the lives of their fellow professionals by revealing to the king his dream and its interpretation.

When the king set up an image in direct contradiction of the dream that he had had, and demanded obedience in bowing down to it, they decided to obey God rather than man and, as a result, experienced a deliverance that astounded the king and the whole nation. Yet since Nebuchadnezzar continued to attribute Babylon's greatness to his own prowess, God once again gave him a dream which Daniel interpreted, and afterward the pagan ruler was finally ready to become a child of God.

Two more incidents complete the story of the first half of the book: God rebuked Belshazzar for his ungodliness and told him that he had lost a kingdom, and Darius the Mede learned that the laws of the Medes and Persians are powerless before the law of God—that God is able to deliver His servant from even the mouths of lions.

The second half of the book contains dreams and visions that reveal to the prophet the future in terms that would be important to him as a man of God. By the same token they are important for us who, like Daniel, want to know what God is going to do about the problem of evil. What will God permit? How long will He allow it to persist? When and how will the righteous be vindicated? It is one thing to know that there will be a succession of kingdoms, but another to know how God's people will be treated and delivered.

Historical Background

Daniel tells us that the vision he received came to him during the first year of the reign of Belshazzar, king of Babylon. Immediately this fact takes us back before the incidents described in the last two chapters. Even before the fall of Babylon and the rise of Medo-Persia, Daniel was seeking to understand the times in which he lived and how God was relating to them.

What were some of the questions that might have entered his mind? He would be concerned about the fulfillment of the dream that came to Nebuchadnezzar, remembering that the ruler had been told, "You are that head of gold" (Dan. 2:38). Did that mean Nebuchadnezzar personally, or his kingdom? We have the answer now, but we have no reason to suppose that Daniel knew precisely. Other kings succeeded Nebuchadnezzar. Did the succession of metals refer to individual kings? Was Belshazzar the fourth king, the fourth metal in the image? If so, then Daniel might have concluded that the release of God's people would be soon.

God graciously gave Daniel a vision so that his mind might be at rest. God treats him not as a servant who does not need to know his master's intentions, but as a friend who can enter into an understanding of His purposes and plans (not completely, of course, because man's limitations make it impossible for him to understand God's ways completely, but with sympathy, because God has given to man memory and reasoning powers, and the means of entering into the relationship of friends).

I am sure that Daniel could see the vast difference between Nebuchadnezzar and his grandson, Belshazzar. The latter showed no interest in doing what was right or learning about the God whom his grandfather had come to know and worship. It may well have been that Daniel was released from his responsibilities at this time. The new ruler did not appreciate his talents. It is understandable that Daniel would ask the question How is God going to handle this situation?

Daniel's Dream and Vision

Now Daniel receives the answer. In a dream—which he knows comes from God—he sees beasts rising out of a sea churned by winds blowing from all four directions.

The first beast is like a lion; the second, a bear; the third, a leopard; and the fourth is indescribable. It has iron teeth and ten horns! Daniel says *like* each time, because the beasts have characteristics that make them different from real animals. The lion has wings and stands up like a man, and it receives a human heart. The bear has three ribs in its mouth. The leopard has four wings and four heads. Obviously the animals are symbolic.

Two parts of the vision so far are striking: first, the beasts originate in the commotion of the sea as it is lashed by four winds and second, they increase in fierceness. The lion has one redeeming feature; it acts like a human being. The bear has three ribs in its mouth and is told, "Get up and eat your fill of flesh" (Dan. 7:5). The leopardlike beast is "given authority to rule" (verse 6). Clearly the creatures possess both authority and cruelty. Arising out of the strife and commotion of world events, they represent what always happens when men are left to their own devices. Such a future has nothing encouraging about it.

Daniel learns that the four beasts represent "four kingdoms that will rise from the earth" (verse 17). In other words, they are human organizations that result from the conflicts of many people. Constantly subject to change, they are just as the waters of a sea blasted by winds from every direction.

No doubt Daniel remembered the image in Nebuchadnezzar's dream and could see a correlation. The lion could very well represent Babylon, the empire that had not yet passed away when Daniel received the vision. Like a lion with wings, Babylon had swiftly extended its authority over the land between the Tigris and Euphrates rivers and conquered Palestine and Egypt. In reference to Babylon, Jeremiah had used the metaphor of a lion when he said, "A lion has come out of his lair; a destroyer of nations has set out" (Jer. 4:7).

The eagle is a majestic bird. For a lion to have the wings of an eagle is to continue the thought of Babylon's greatness. But those wings were to be removed, and doubtless Daniel saw the change that took place in Babylon as a conquering power. The lion ceased to act as a lion when it began to stand up like a man, and it lost the characteristics of a lion when it received the heart of a man. It is one thing for a man to have the heart of a lion, but an entirely different thing for a lion to have the heart of a man.

The Hebrew prophet would agree that the Babylon he saw under Nebuchadnezzar differed greatly from the empire under the king's successors. Daniel may well have regretted the change, because while Nebuchadnezzar had come to recognize God's authority and was willing to accept advice from the Hebrew captive who held high office in the government, his successors knew only violence and court intrigue and had rejected the prophet as an adviser.

If we accept the date of this vision as being in 550/549 B.C., as Gerhard Hasel has shown in his study of recent archaeological findings (*Andrews University Seminary Studies*, Autumn 1977, p. 167), then we may be sure that Daniel knew nothing of the application of the symbol of the bear to the Medo-Persian Empire; but he may have known of the rise to power of Cyrus II of Anshan and of his successful revolt against his father-in-law, Astyages, entering Ecbatana, the Median king's capital, in triumph in 550 B.C. If any threat faced Babylon, it would come from the East.

He would also know, as a devout Jew having access to the writings of the prophets, that Isaiah had prophesied about a Cyrus who would say about Jerusalem, "Let it be rebuilt" (Isa. 44:28). Nothing would have pleased him better than to know that within a lifetime his city would be rebuilt. But he would read on in the prophecy and learn that Babylon would fall (Isa. 45:1). Would Medo-Persia conquer Babylon? Daniel did not know then because this vision was before the fulfillment of prophecy. But the events taking place around him—compared with Scripture—would give him an inkling.

We must always be careful how we interpret unfulfilled prophecy. Only when it comes to completion can we be sure of the interpretation. In this respect we have a great advantage over Daniel—we can see what he could never have, except in symbol.

But Daniel's attention seems to have riveted on the fourth beast, singling it out for interpretation (Dan. 7:19). Perhaps its power to do damage—the way it "trampled underfoot whatever was left" after it had broken things in pieces—impressed him. Could any temporal power be more devastating than the powers he had already seen? The prospect was certainly fearsome. Then he wondered about the horns, 10 of them! If one could do so much damage, and if two could double the trouble, what about 10?

Then he thought of the horn that uprooted three others in its growth. Not only more imposing than the others, it had eyes and spoke boastfully. Declaring war against the saints, it began "defeating them" (verse 21). Here was a matter for great concern. Why would God allow such a thing to take place? Daniel could understand the Exile. In no way saints, his people deserved it. But why would the Lord permit the saints to be defeated? It seemed totally foreign to God's way. People always ask why bad things happen to good people? Why the Holocaust? If God is in control, why does evil appear to triumph? Such questions are not always easy to answer, but we must face them. And the answer is in this very chapter!

The twenty-second verse begins with the word *until*. It points to a time when a change will take place. God is patient, and we must learn to be patient too!

The Judgment Scene

When Daniel describes the judgment scene he uses the language of poetry:

"Thrones were set in place,
and the Ancient of Days took his seat" (verse 9).

By using the word *thrones* Daniel suggests that we have here no ordinary scene. Thrones are the seats of kings and judges. By referring to God as "the Ancient of Days" he is letting us know that God exists from eternity and will continue for an eternity to come. The Lord is the source of all being and the ultimate reality. Yet He is not some impersonal force, for He takes His seat.

Daniel continues his description in terms that we can understand, in human language. He refers to God's clothing as "white as snow," suggesting to us absolute purity—no contamination whatever. His hair is "white as wool," implying age and patriarchal authority, but more importantly, wisdom. God is acquainted with everything that is past. He is aware of everything that awaits us in the present. And He knows what to do in the present so that the future can be glorious. His throne is flaming fire, indicating that He transcends all that is human. Fire burns up dross, purifying a substance. The symbol emphasizes God's absolute purity. The wheels suggest mobility. Not limited to only one place, God can be anywhere and everywhere.

A river of fire proceeds out of His presence. Nothing that is impure can come before Him. Moses had a similar conception of God when he said, "Be careful not to forget the covenant of the Lord your God that he made with you; do not make for yourselves an idol in the form of anything the Lord your God has forbidden. For the Lord your God is a consuming fire, a jealous God" (Deut. 4:23, 24).

Daniel goes on to say that "thousands upon thousands attended him," an innumerable throng, all ready to serve God. "Ten thousand times ten thousand stood before him." As Paul says, "We will all stand before God's judgment seat" (Rom. 14:10). "The court was seated, and the books were opened." Solemnly a cosmic hearing convenes.

Now Daniel's attention reverts to the earth, and he sees that eventually "the beast was slain and its body destroyed and thrown into the blazing fire" (Dan. 7:11). Clearly the God of heaven, the Judge of all the earth, has pronounced His final verdict, and sentence has been executed. Such a moment is one of sadness, yet it is also a time of joy, because God has taken action to destroy evil.

But the prophet looks to heaven again, and there he sees "one like a son of man, coming with the clouds of heaven" (verse 13). The being "approached the Ancient of Days and was led into his presence." Daniel used that same word *like* in connection with the beasts. No doubt he felt impressed with the difference between "beast" on the one hand and "son of man" on the other. The beasts represented fierce and dominating kingdoms of human origin. By contrast, the "son of man" would receive a kingdom of divine origin. "He was given authority, glory and sovereign power." But more importantly, "all peoples, nations, and men of every language worshiped him." Not surprisingly "his dominion is an everlasting dominion that will not pass away, and his kingdom is one that will never be destroyed" (verse 14).

Son of Man
Did Daniel know who this Son of man might be? The

term *son of man* could refer to a human being. Thus God addressed Ezekiel as "son of man" (eg. Eze. 2:1; 4:1; 5:1; 6:1). The prophet would also know that God had created man in His image and given him dominion over all the earth (Gen. 1:26). But Adam had failed to fulfill God's plans for him. Sin entered the world, and with sin, death. Yet God was looking for those who would recognize His Lordship, and from time to time some, like Abraham, believed the divine promises of salvation, and it was credited to them as righteousness (Gen. 15:6; Rom. 4:3).

Kingship in Israel was to represent a relationship between the human ruler and Yahweh. The king would be a son to God the Father (2 Sam. 7:14). The king on earth would recognize the sovereignty of the God of heaven. Unfortunately Israel's leaders did not always fulfill their primary role, but God promised that one would come who would honor it completely. Called "Mighty God" (Isa. 9:6), He would deserve and receive worship. Did Daniel recognize all this?

Daniel did understand that Nebuchadnezzar, as ruler in Babylon, needed to submit to the sovereignty of God. After the interpretation of the first dream Nebuchadnezzar acknowledged Daniel's God as "Lord of kings" (Dan. 2:47). With the second dream Nebuchadnezzar knew "that the Most High is sovereign over the kingdoms of men and gives them to anyone he wishes" (Dan. 4:17). Robert D. Rowe observed that: "Nebuchadnezzar had to acknowledge that his authority as king was not supreme; it was subject to God's kingship, which made demands both upon his conduct and his attitude" ("Is Daniel's 'Son of Man' Messianic?" in Harold M. Rowden, ed., *Christ the Lord: Studies in Christology Presented to Donald Guthrie* [Chicago: Inter-Varsity Press, 1982], p. 84).

Hence we may conclude that Daniel would have an inkling as to the meaning of "son of man," but it is for us who live after the times of Jesus that the connection is unmistakable. Jesus often referred to Himself as the Son of man. In using the title He was no doubt calling attention to the book of Daniel. Note the high priest's question and how Jesus answered it in Matthew 26:63, 64. The reference seems to suggest that He equated "Son of man" with "Son of God." (See also Luke 22:69, 70; Mark 14:61, 62.) Jesus seems to have avoided the title Christ, probably because the Jews had misconceptions regarding the Messiah's function and He did not want to be associated with such concepts (Matt. 16:20).

Time of the Judgment

Even though Daniel may not have had a complete understanding of his dream, he must have noticed that the judgment came after the fourth beast had arrived on the scene, after the appearance of the 10 horns and after the rise of the horn that spoke boastfully. In fact, it would occur after the horn tried to change set times and laws and after it had dominated the saints for a "time, times and half a time." Daniel tells us that his thoughts left him "deeply troubled," and no doubt he could not understand many aspects of the vision. Here is where those of us who live two thousand five hundred years after the time of Daniel have an advantage. We can see how history has confirmed the vision in many details.

Now we know that Medo-Persia succeeded Babylon, Greece replaced Medo-Persia, and Rome followed Greece. When Rome fell to the barbarians, Europe shattered into a number of major kingdoms. We also know that "out of the ruins of political Rome, arose the great moral Empire in the 'giant form' of the Roman Church" (A. C. Flick, *The Rise of the Mediaeval Church*, p. 150, *The SDA Bible Commentary*, vol. 4, p. 826). The Papacy proved to be a power as great as any of the other horns, but it was different in the sense that it was basically an ecclesiastical organization rather than a purely political entity.

History also tells us that the influence of the bishop of Rome rose when Justinian recognized his primacy and the

Ostrogoths went down to defeat in A.D. 538. For 1260 years the papacy was in power, until in 1798, General Berthier, under orders from Napoleon, took the pope prisoner. This period is what Daniel saw in vision as "time, times and half a time," an interval during which many Christian groups experienced persecution.

"But the court will sit, and his power will be taken away and completely destroyed forever" (Dan. 7:26). God makes His decision. "Then the sovereignty, power and greatness of the kingdoms under the whole heaven will be handed over to the saints, the people of the Most High. His kingdom will be an everlasting kingdom, and all rulers will worship and obey him" (verse 27). That is your prospect and mine, by God's grace. The past may be prologue, but the future is fulfillment.

Daniel kept the matter to himself (verse 28) because he still had many unanswered questions. But for us the situation is different. We see prophecy fulfilled, and we know the future is certain. Thank God we can face the future with confidence.

PRINCIPLES OF LIFE

Do you agree that the following propositions are principles that arise out of a study of Scripture and that we need to apply them in our lives?

1. We should not be upset because of the prosperity of the wicked (Ps. 37). Their doom is sealed. Our duty is to trust in God and to do what is right, regardless of our circumstances.

2. The wicked have everything to fear in the judgment, but Christians who have an advocate with the Father have nothing to fear (Isa. 43:25; Matt. 10:32, 33).

3. God may seem to take a long time before He acts, but we may be sure that His timing is for the best. No one will be able to say, "I did not know. I had no chance."

4. God will triumph in the end, and His people with Him. It is for us to be patient and to persevere in doing what is right.

5. Man is free to do what he wants to do with his life, but he must be prepared to take the consequences if he makes the wrong choices.

6. Only God is in a position to judge, because He alone has all the evidence to make the right evaluations. Man should refrain from judging anyone except himself.

7. To refrain from judging someone is not to avoid deciding what is right and what is wrong. God's Word is a lamp that lights up the hidden recesses of the heart and makes clear the way we should go.

8. God prefers enlightened obedience to blind submission. That is why He treats us as friends and reveals His plans and purposes.

9. When God gives us a revelation, He also assures us of its divine origin, so that we may have no doubt as to proper guidance.

WORTH NOTING:

"Every man's work passes in review before God and is registered for faithfulness or unfaithfulness. Opposite each name in the books of heaven is entered with terrible exactness every wrong word, every selfish act, every unfulfilled duty, and every secret sin, with every artful dissembling. Heaven-sent warnings or reproofs neglected, wasted moments, unimproved opportunities, the influence exerted for good or for evil, with its far-reaching results, all are chronicled by the recording angel" (*The Great Controversy*, p. 482).

"All who have truly repented of sin, and by faith claimed the blood of Christ as their atoning sacrifice, have had pardon entered against their names in the books of heaven" (*ibid.*, p. 483).

Prophetic Update:
A Matter of Time

"The light that Daniel received direct from God was given especially for these last days. The visions he saw by the banks of the Ulai [chapter 8] and the Hiddekel [chapter 10], the great rivers of Shinar, are now in process of fulfillment, and all the events foretold will soon have come to pass" (Ellen G. White letter 57, 1896).

Introduction

Daniel began the book in Hebrew, but in the second chapter broke off into Aramaic when he started to tell about the Chaldeans who addressed King Nebuchadnezzar with the wish "O king, live forever." He continued with Aramaic until the beginning of chapter 8.

Why did he use two languages? Daniel does not tell us, but we may presume that he was proficient in both languages and used the one or the other according to need. As we look at the subject matter in Aramaic and Hebrew, it would seem that Daniel addressed his fellow Jews in Hebrew—many of them not being familiar with the Aramaic—and wrote in Aramaic when the subject matter suited the Babylonians, most of whom did not know Hebrew. Also he quotes from official documents that were probably written in Aramaic, the official language of government correspondence.

Daniel dates chapter 8 in the third year of King Belshazzar, meaning that two years had passed since the vision of the seventh chapter. But seven or eight years would still pass before Babylon would fall to the Medes and Persians.

The new vision of chapter eight suggests that Daniel continued to have problems understanding the future. Concerned about his people still in exile, he worried that Jerusalem yet remained in ruins. He still remembered the siege of Jerusalem in 597 B.C., when Nebuchadnezzar's forces took Jehoiachin captive to Babylon and placed Zedekiah on the throne, and the final overthrow of Jerusalem in 586 B.C. How did the vision he had received two years previously relate to his people? We know that he still has that vision in mind because he refers to it in the first verse of this chapter with the words "after the one that had already appeared to me." It would be interesting to see how the new vision complemented the old, how Daniel received further insights so that he might know what to expect.

The Vision

Daniel sees himself in a new location. He is not in Babylon, the capital of Babylonia, but Susa, "in the province of Elam." The prophet is close now to the Persia of Cyrus the Great, who in 547 B.C. had overcome Croesus and his Lydian kingdom. Did Daniel make a connection between him and the Cyrus mentioned by Isaiah as rebuilding Jerusalem (Isa. 44:28; 45:1)? While we need not suppose that Daniel was less interested in watching prophecy being fulfilled than we are today; I believe he was more cautious in making predictions than some of us. That is why he was never dogmatic except in matters that were definitely revealed.

In vision the prophet stands on the banks of the Ulai Canal. Glancing around, he observes a ram. Here we begin with symbolic language. The ram has two horns, one longer than the other (KJV says "higher"). Usually a ram has two equal-length horns, but this is a symbolic animal. Later he would learn that "the two-horned ram that you saw represents the kings of Media and Persia" (Dan. 8:20). Daniel would understand that Persia came to power after Media, and Cyrus the Great rebelled and overcame the Median king, Astyages, in 550 B.C. Persia grew up later.

The ram charged in three significant directions—west, north, and south—which would fit in well with the history of the spread of Medo-Persia. The empire develops unhindered. "No animal could stand against him" (verse 4). Furthermore, the symbolic beast did as he pleased. That is the trouble with all earthly powers. They do not do what God desires, nor do they ask what He wants. Whether nations or individuals, decline or calamity is the inevitable result.

"Suddenly a goat" appears on the scene. A "prominent horn" between the eyes, it comes flying from the west—flying because it does not seem to touch the ground. Seeing the ram, it attacks with great fury, shattering the horns of the ram. It throws the helpless ram to the ground and tramples it. No one comes to the ram's aid. While it is now the goat's turn to become great, a surprising thing happens: the prominent horn breaks off right in the midst of power and prosperity. And in its place arise four prominent horns pointing in four different directions.

Daniel discovers that the shaggy goat represents Greece, and the prominent horn is the first king, obviously Alexander the Great. We all know not only the speed of his conquests but also that he died in the prime of his life and career. As for the generals who succeeded him, they divided the empire among themselves, first into four and then into three major parts.

Verse 9 in Daniel's story we must read with care. It is easy to misunderstand the statement "Out of one of them." Out of one of what? We could imagine that it means one of the four horns. Actually, though, it refers to something coming out of one of the four winds mentioned in the previous verse. A careful study of the Hebrew indicates that this must be the case, because of the use of gender in the Hebrew. Horns are feminine in gender, and winds can be feminine or masculine. Since the word for "them" is masculine, it cannot refer to "horns" but must point back to "winds."

The issue is important because it affects interpretation. Those who assume that the horn of verse 9 arises out of one of the horns of verse 8 must look for a fulfillment in connection with one of the four parts of Alexander's empire as divided among the generals. Those who recognize that the horn of verse 9 originates from one of the winds, or directions, of verse 8 can see how Rome, advancing from the west—independently of the divisions of the Grecian empire—fits the appropriateness of the expansion of this horn to the south, to the east, and to the "Beautiful Land."

Palestine is appropriately called the beautiful, pleasant, or glorious land. In Old Testament times it carried the title of the "land flowing with milk and honey" (Ex. 3:8).

One can see a pattern in this vision similar to that of the dreams of Daniel 2 and 7. Kingdom follows kingdom. In Daniel 2 and 7 the first kingdom is Babylon, but in Daniel 8, the first kingdom is Medo-Persia. This is understandable because Daniel is close to Medo-Persia in location and time. Since the kingdom that followed Greece is Rome, we may expect Rome to come after Greece in the vision of Daniel 8. Commentators suggest that this is Rome in both its pagan and papal phases.

What is more important to note is the power's activity. "It grew until it reached the host of the heavens, and it threw some of the starry host down to the earth and trampled on them" (Dan. 9:10). Like those before it, the new empire does not acknowledge God's sovereignty. It does not recognize those who worship the true God. The interpretation in verse 24 refers to the "holy people" as being the objects of attack. Nor is it afraid to compare itself with the "Prince of the host" (verse 11). In verse 25 we learn that the power takes a stand against the "Prince of princes." This can mean only Christ, who suffered under Pontius Pilate. The Roman official found no fault in Jesus but still delivered Him to be crucified in order to pacify a hostile mob (Matt. 27:11-26).

"It took away the daily sacrifice from him, and the place of his sanctuary was brought low" (verse 11). Here is another verse that needs careful study. Commentators have offered different interpretations. Even Adventist scholars have not been united in its meaning. One of the problems—and perhaps the major one—is that the Hebrew text is not absolutely clear. In such cases dogmatism is out of order. For example, the Hebrew word translated "daily sacrifice" is one word meaning daily or continual. "Sacrifice" is added as interpretation. Does the word mean the long continuance of Satan's opposition to the work of Christ through the medium of paganism as some aver, or is it the continual priestly ministry of Christ in the heavenly sanctuary as others would insist? The latest Adventist writer on the subject believes that the *daily* refers to "true worship" (cf. C. M. Maxwell, *God Cares*, pp. 156-166).

The SDA Bible Commentary declares: "Perhaps this is one of the passages of Scripture on which we must wait until a better day for a final answer" (vol. 4, p. 843). All the same, we may be sure that Rome, in both its pagan and papal phases, has opposed true worship, whether by imposing the worship of the emperor or by setting up practices and teaching doctrines that the Scriptures do not sanction. The Christian must always be on his guard against false teaching. Human organizations will always have some aspect that will not be in harmony with biblical principles. Thus the Christian will always be on guard to obey God rather than men.

The word *sanctuary* must have instantly caught the prophet's attention. His thoughts would go immediately to Jerusalem, where the Temple lay in ruins. How long would it stay in that condition? How long would it remain desecrated? He listened carefully as two saints entered into conversation, and one of them asked the question he had in his own mind. Then the answer came, and Daniel recorded it in verse 14. "It will take 2,300 evenings and mornings; then the sanctuary will be reconsecrated."

The expression "evening and morning" would have been familiar to him from the first chapter of Genesis where evening and morning constituted one day. He knew that 2,300 evenings and mornings would mean 2,300 days.

Of course, Gabriel, who was his interpreter, had said that the vision concerned "the time of the end" (verse 17). Would the sanctuary really remain desecrated to the end of time? Such thoughts and questions must have troubled Daniel considerably. He says that while Gabriel was speaking to him he was in a deep sleep and lying facedown. Then the angel touched him and raised him to his feet (verse 18).

It is interesting to note that a human being, even a man of God like Daniel, finds communication with heavenly beings stressful. We do not always recognize the limitations of human nature. Fortunately angels, when they appear to human beings—as they often do to protect them from danger—do so as human beings. Often we do not realize that it was an angel that we entertained, or who joined us in our travels. We must always recognize the vast difference between sinful man and a holy being.

Now Gabriel tells him "what will happen later in the time of wrath, because the vision concerns the appointed time of the end" (verse 19). God saw fit to reveal to Daniel a long-range program so that his record would be of value not only in his day but also in our own. A great controversy rages between the forces of evil and of good, between Christ and Satan. Again and again it will appear as though evil has triumphed. But God is in control, and we may be sure that His truth will win.

After Gabriel describes the cunning and deceitful practices of an empire like Rome, he assures Daniel that the kingdom "will be destroyed, but not by human power" (verse 25). Human effort does not bring about reform or change for the better. Man lost his ability to do good when he yielded himself to Satan. Only God's re-creative power, only His grace, can transform a world situation. God will enable those who take His side to do good, but those who persist in evil, who reject Him and His government, will always be evil. The time will come when God says, "Enough!" Every man will then have made his irrevocable decision. And God will destroy the evil and set up His eternal kingdom of truth and righteousness. "Today, if you hear his voice, do not harden your hearts" (Heb. 3:7, 8).

Daniel receives a final word: "The vision of the evenings and mornings that has been given you is true" (Dan. 8:26). Whatever may be his reaction to the time involved, he must know that it is true. But its secret is still sealed. Neither Daniel nor his fellow countrymen can understand it because it has to do with an event in the distant future.

Exhausted, Daniel lay ill for several days. The vision appalled him—"it was beyond understanding" (verse 27). Little did he know at the time that further light would come, as we know it did. Many aspects of truth are difficult for the human mind to grasp. Paul once commented about the great "mystery of godliness" (1 Tim. 3:16). The Incarnation, the death on the cross, the empty tomb—these are only three of the intricacies of our religion. But we must not let go of God simply because we cannot fathom His ways, nor must our faith weaken when things happen to us and our friends that we cannot explain. For example, His coming may seem delayed, but it is sure. We place our trust in God; He will not let us down.

PRINCIPLES OF LIFE

Here are some more propositions for your consideration. Do they seem to you to be in harmony with the teaching of the Bible?

1. We cannot always expect immediate responses from God. The time might not yet be right for Him to speak or act. Therefore we must leave it to God to decide when it is appropriate to give us an answer.

2. The way we live today determines where we shall be

in the future, and for both the present and the future we depend on God's grace.

3. "The secret things belong to the Lord our God, but the things revealed belong to us and to our children forever, that we may follow all the words of [God's] law" (Deut. 29:29).

4. The Christian may expect persecution, but he must not seek it out!

5. The prophet does not always understand what God has revealed to him, because prophecy is best understood when fulfilled.

6. We must always appreciate the difference between us and the angels and between us and God. It is an awesome experience to come into His presence, and we must do so with proper respect and decorum.

WORTH NOTING:

"A careful study of the working out of God's purpose in the history of nations and in the revelation of things to come, will help us to estimate at their true value things seen and things unseen, and to learn what is the true aim of life. Thus viewing the things of time in the light of eternity, we may, like Daniel and his fellows, live for that which is true and noble and enduring. And learning in this life the principles of the kingdom of our Lord and Saviour, that blessed kingdom which is to endure for ever and ever, we may be prepared at His coming to enter with Him into its possession" *(Prophets and Kings*, p. 548).

Daniel Prays: God Adds Further Light

"Daniel's example of prayer and confession is given for our instruction and encouragement.... Daniel knew that the appointed time for Israel's captivity was nearly ended; but he did not feel that because God had promised to deliver them, they themselves had no part to act" (Review and Herald, *Feb. 9, 1897, in* The SDA Bible Commentary, *vol. 4, p. 1172).*

The Time

Daniel tells us that the events he reports in the ninth chapter of his book took place during the "first year of Darius son of Xerxes (a Mede by descent), who was made ruler over the Babylonian kingdom" (verse 1). That would be in 538 B.C., the year after the fall of Babylon.

Nearly 10 years had passed since the vision recorded in chapter 8. Gabriel had not fully explained it, however, because, for one thing, it concerned the distant future and, for another, Daniel had become exhausted, collapsing into an illness that lasted several days. Clearly communication with heaven and with heavenly beings can drain one's nervous energy. Furthermore, Daniel was now in his late 70s, and the strain would be even greater on him. But perhaps his great concern was the restoration of the sanctuary from its defiled state to a condition that would permit proper worship. The period of "2,300 evenings and mornings," which would need to pass before he and his people could contemplate any change, was overwhelming. Yet he had been assured by the angel Gabriel that the vision was true in this respect.

Bible Study and Research

After a comparatively short illness, the prophet went about the king's business, which may have been only peripheral governmental duties, since Belshazzar probably did not want to have anything to do with the Judean captive who had been so influential on his grandfather Nebuchadnezzar.

With lessened responsibility in the government, Daniel set about studying the sacred writings to discover and understand God's principles and purposes. We may be sure that he had access to and studied that portion of Scripture called the Torah, the first five books of Moses. He could refer to the historical writings of the early prophets, books written by Samuel, Nathan, and Gad. Thus he would know the history of the kings of Israel and Judah, about King Hezekiah and the prophet Isaiah, who had tried to keep the Hebrew rulers going straight. Also he would know about Jeremiah and his problems in Jerusalem. It would be strange if he did not know about Ezekiel, the priest whom God used as a prophet by the river Chebar in Babylonia. As a government official, Daniel was well aware of the fall of Jerusalem in 597 B.C. and then its destruction in 586 B.C., and would know of the captives brought to Babylon. He had been a part of these events. He might have met many of them and discussed matters of mutual concern, such as the state of worship in Jerusalem.

One thing is sure: he continued to pray regularly with his windows open toward Jerusalem. Having a strong belief that the captivity would not last forever—even though it was well deserved—he would long for the day when true worship would resume at the site that Yahweh had chosen as the place of meeting for His people.

Already nearly 70 years had passed since he and his

young companions had been taken captive in 605 B.C. How much longer would it be? He may have given up hope of his ever returning to Jerusalem, but he did want his people—God's people—to repent and return to the old city, to the land that God had given them.

He had already seen Babylon fall, interpreted the dream of Nebuchadnezzar recorded in Daniel 2, and witnessed the partial fulfillment of his own dream recorded in Daniel 7. The prophecy of Isaiah must have impressed him: "Go down, sit in the dust, Virgin Daughter of Babylon; sit on the ground without a throne, Daughter of the Babylonians. No more will you be called tender or delicate" (Isa. 47:1). Emphatically he would agree with verse 6: "I [God] was angry with my people and desecrated my inheritance; I gave them into your [Babylonia's] hand, and you showed them no mercy." Daniel would remember the image of gold as he read the words: "You said, 'I will continue forever—the eternal queen!' But you did not consider these things or reflect on what might happen" (verse 7).

I can see Daniel smile as he thinks of his student days in the University of Babylon and reads: "Keep on, then, with your magic spells and with your many sorceries, which you have labored at since childhood. Perhaps you will succeed, perhaps you will cause terror. All the counsel you have received has only worn you out! Let your astrologers come forward, those stargazers who make predictions month by month, let them save you from what is coming upon you" (Isa. 47:12, 13). Of course he had long considered much of Babylon's learning useless.

Many years earlier the prophet Isaiah had written "an oracle concerning Babylon," in which God had said: "See, I will stir up against them the Medes" (Isa. 13:17). He would say amen to verse 19: "Babylon, the jewel of kingdoms, the glory of the Babylonians' pride, will be overthrown by God." It was God who was at work in the rise and fall of kingdoms. National prosperity or decline had little to do with human prowess, although God uses man as the instrument of His purposes. Isaiah expressed it quite well: "For the Lord Almighty has purposed, and who can thwart him? His hand is stretched out, and who can turn it back?" (Isa. 14:27).

Perhaps one of Isaiah's most outstanding prophecies was the particular reference to Cyrus (Isa. 44:28). Daniel had heard of Cyrus and his success against Croesus of Lydia. Some parts of the prophecy were still incomplete, but the coming to pass of part made the fulfillment of the rest practically certain. Daniel would agree with the prophet's reference to the Babylonian gods in Isaiah 46:1, 2, and would remember clearly the story of Hezekiah in Isaiah 38 and 39, with its prophecy in which Daniel himself was part of the fulfillment (Isa. 39:7).

The Jews in Exile

The Jews in exile probably had mixed feelings about their stay in Babylonia. They no doubt missed the often rocky and terraced terrain of Palestine. The land between the rivers Tigris and Euphrates was rich and fertile, well watered with rivers and canals, affording plenty of work and food. But the climate was dry and hot and dusty, and the terrain largely flat. In this respect it was not as attractive as their Palestine with its hills and valleys, its regular seasons of rain, and its variety of fruits. Many were homesick, and as they met together to discuss the good old days, they would recall the songs of Zion, although not in a mood to sing them. They hung their harps on poplar trees, and wept (Ps. 137).

But others were impressed with the splendor of the city of Babylon, its magnificent Istar Gate, its Procession Street with gorgeous parades, its complex of temples in the Esagila, and above all, its palaces and the Hanging Gardens. The marketplaces afforded opportunities for trade. Babylon was a political center. Government officials and representatives from many parts of the empire came to it, all seeking information, all exploiting its wealth in one way or another.

Many Jews would have mingled with the crowds. The

empire allowed them to colonize in Babylonia wherever they wished. Some artisans and craftsmen whom Nebuchadnezzar had chosen especially for his many building enterprises pursued skills they had developed in their home country. Many worked at farming, irrigation, and construction. There was no unemployment. The men bought land and built houses and settled down with their families. Young people married and had children. Some Jews, like Daniel and his friends, occupied high positions in the government.

The Jews by the river Chebar had a priest in their midst whom God had used also as a prophet, namely, Ezekiel. The exiles experienced no religious persecution, no interference with religious practices. Scholars could pursue their studies and do their teaching. The devout among them met on the Sabbath—not for a ceremonial service, such as would be the case in the Temple, but to read and hear the Scriptures, to discuss their religious interests, and to pray. Thus the institution of the synagogue began to emerge. Daniel doubtless took advantage of such occasions to share his visions with others.

While many became rich and prosperous, many also continued to ask what would happen to Jerusalem and the Temple. They wondered whether God had forsaken them, whether indeed the gods of the Babylonians were more powerful than Yahweh. But Daniel knew that God had been in control all the time. The only thing was that he could not always understand divine maneuverings. At times God's plan seemed terribly slow in its implementation. Perhaps he should do something about it. Yes, he would pray!

Lessons of the Captivity

The Exile had not been a total disaster. Had not Nebuchadnezzar become a child of God? Had not Darius come to realize that the God of Daniel was the living God, the One who rescues and saves, the One who endures forever? (Dan. 6:26, 27). Had not the miracle of the fiery furnace been a tremendous witness not only to the faithfulness of three Hebrews but also to the mighty power of the God of the Hebrews? In spite of His people's failings, a knowledge of the true God had spread to the surrounding world.

If the Jews had learned anything, it was the utter futility of worshiping idols. They would never go back to idolatry. Now they found mutual comfort and strength in the synagogue. They discoverd that the spiritual life need not depend on rites and ceremonies, but was a product of a right relationship with God. Furthermore, they came to value their sacred writings, the teachings of the Torah. Being strangers in a foreign country, they had learned to be more united as a community. And last but not least, they had realized that they could worship their God anywhere, because He was the one true God who was near all; none, whether Jew or Gentile, could escape from his or her responsibility to Him.

Daniel's Prayer

Daniel approached God with wholehearted devotion. To indicate his seriousness, he fasted in sackcloth and ashes. With abject humility he came to God as a suppliant, declaring that he had read the Scriptures and understood that God had decreed that the Captivity in Babylon would not last more than 70 years, and the 70 years were just about ended. Of course, he realized that the fulfillment of the prophecy might depend upon whether the hearts of the people were right with God. Wanting to be right with God for himself, he knew it called for confession of sin, and he did so, including his own sins and those of the people.

Let us notice some of the phrases:

"The great and awesome God" (Dan. 9:4). We must never forget His transcendence, the vast difference between Him and ourselves. We view those who hold high office with respect and deference even though they are human. How much more should we, putting all frivolity aside, approach

God with a sense of His dignity.

"Who keeps his covenant of love with all who love him and obey his commands." Nothing can separate us from the love of God (Rom. 8:35-39). We can estrange ourselves from Him only by our disobedience. How foolish it is for us to live our lives contrary to God's will when we know that by doing it we can enjoy satisfaction in this life and eternal happiness in the world to come.

"We have sinned" (Dan. 9:5). Can anyone say anything different? Yet the outlook is not hopeless. We may have our sins forgiven through the plan of salvation, which God has outlined for us.

"We have not listened to your servants the prophets" (verse 6). None of us has read the Scriptures as diligently as we might have done. We have preferred to go our own way. Perhaps we did not want to be told the right way lest we feel obliged to follow it!

"Lord, you are righteous" (verse 7). This can be a frightening aspect of His character except as we remember that His righteousness makes us righteous.

"The Lord our God is merciful and forgiving" (verse 9). Not an excuse to continue in sin, rather it is a reason to forsake it. It is a terrible crime to presume on God's mercy.

"Just as it is written in the Law of Moses" (verse 13). The Word of God helps us understand ourselves and the world around us. It points up weaknesses in our character and tells us how to make changes.

"For your sake, O Lord" (verse 17). Here is our only effective plea, for we have no merits of our own. We can be thankful that we have a God whose only desire is for us to escape the

destruction of this world and be saved in His eternal kingdom.

God's Response

Daniel's prayer indicates that His main concern has to do with the desolate sanctuary and the city of Jerusalem. God's response indicates that while the earthly Jerusalem and its Temple were important, the coming of the Messiah was even *more* vital.

The earthly Jerusalem could be rebuilt. But what was to guarantee that it would never face destruction or desecration again? The Jewish captives could go back to their city and country, but how could one be sure that they would not fall into the sins of their forefathers?

Perhaps Daniel's prayer indicates that we human beings have small visions, however right they may be. But God sees far beyond the immediate present. While the prophet was thinking in terms of 70 years, God was dealing with 70 times 7! Daniel worried about the welfare of his own people, while God had in mind the welfare of the whole world, the destiny of Jews and Gentiles as determined by the coming of the Anointed One, the Messiah. In the ninth chapter of the book of Daniel we find the center of all prophecy—that is—in terms of the New Testament—Jesus Christ.

Did Daniel grasp the full impact of what he was hearing? Probably not! Not even the greatest minds can comprehend the magnitude of God's truth. But the prophet did understand some important matters. As he prayed God was sending the answer. "As soon as you began to pray, an answer was given" (verse 23). God knows our innermost thoughts before we express them. Our language may be halting, wholly inadequate for the occasion, but the Lord ignores such externals. He knows what we desire, and He gives us more than we ask for. Can we wish for any greater or more-caring God?

How often we feel as though our prayers rise no higher than the ceiling. It seems as though we have to wait forever for the reply. But the fact is that before we speak, God has an answer. While the answer may not be what we have asked for, it is always something that is best for us. We may not recognize the answer, but it is there all the same. How grateful we should be that God responds, not in the limited way that our mind works, but in the unlimited ways of His grace.

Gabriel said that he had come to give Daniel "insight and understanding." Both qualities are important. Insight lets us in to the secrets of God's plans, while understanding helps us to face life's problems with confidence. Insight lets us know that we are not alone in this world, having to fight the forces of evil in our own strength. Understanding keeps us calm when calamities strike, when things that we cannot explain happen to us.

Gabriel said that Daniel was "highly esteemed." We can see why. In many respects he has set us an example. And studying Daniel's life, we can recognize what we need to do if we are also to be highly esteemed in the sight of Heaven. God does not view our struggles lightly. He always looks down with favor on those who, like Daniel, wish only to do what is right.

The Revelation

"Seventy 'sevens' are decreed for your people" (verse 24). Gabriel seems to begin his message rather abruptly, but we should know that he is referring to the vision in Daniel 8, seeking to add light to what was left unexplained at that time. It was obvious that the prophet was concerned about the 2300-day/year period. Did it mean that the captivity would continue beyond the 70 years of Jeremiah's prophecy? Daniel hoped not, and he prayed for forgiveness so that God would not have to extend the period.

The angel told him that 490 years were "marked out" (NEB) for his people. That is, a period of 490 years would be allotted to the Jewish nation, a time span that would begin with "the issuing of the decree to restore and rebuild

Jerusalem" (verse 25). Being "marked out," or "cut off" as the Hebrew word indicates, means that the shorter period would be part of the larger one. That is, the 490 years would form the first part of the 2300-day/year period. Now that we know when the shorter period begins, we know when the longer one commences.

Ezra gives us a copy of the decree of Artaxerxes authorizing the Jews to return and rebuild Jerusalem (Ezra 7:12-26). He tells us that it was during the king's seventh year of reign that he arrived in Jerusalem for his task (verse 8). Summarizing the various forces that led to the rebuilding, he declares, "So the elders of the Jews continued to build and prosper under the preaching of Haggai the prophet and Zechariah, a descendant of Iddo. They finished building the Temple according to the command of the God of Israel and the decrees of Cyrus, Darius and Artaxerxes, kings of Persia" (Ezra 6:14). History tells us that the issuing of the decree took place in the year 457 B.C.

But our chief concern must be with what happens at the end of the 490-year period. In Daniel 9:24 Gabriel mentions six things:

1. *"To finish transgression."* By the end of this period the Israelites would have finally decided their attitude toward God's leadership. God could not forever extend grace to a people determined to reject His warnings.

2. *"To put an end to sin."* With Christ as the sin-bearer, there would be no need for sin offerings in Temple services. Type would meet antitype.

3. *"To atone for wickedness."* Jesus on the cross made atonement for sin. He said, "But I, when I am lifted up from the earth, will draw all men to myself" (John 12:32).

4. *"To bring in everlasting righteousness."* Jesus died on the cross not only to forgive sin but also to be able to impute and impart His righteousness to all who will accept His offer.

5. *"To seal up vision and prophecy."* That is, to ratify the vision so that by the fulfillment of one part we may be sure that the other parts will be fulfilled as well.

6. *"To anoint the most holy."* This must refer to the sanctuary in heaven and not on earth. It points to the time when Christ is inaugurated as high priest to conduct His high-priestly functions in the courts of heaven. Gabriel divides the 490 years into three parts: "seven 'sevens'"; "sixty-two 'sevens'"; and "one 'seven.'" The Messiah, or Anointed One (Christ), confirms a covenant with many for one "seven," and in the middle of the "seven" period "he will put an end to sacrifice and offering" (verse 27). Also "after the sixty-two 'sevens,' the Anointed One will be cut off." This clearly alludes to His death.

It takes a little concentration to work out all the details, and one must admit that the Hebrew is not always as clear as it might be, leading to a number of different English translations, but the thrust of the prophecy is clear: God's purpose for the salvation of His people cannot be accomplished by the blood of animals (Heb. 10:11, 12). Only Jesus, by His death on the cross, could do that. Hence God is telling Daniel that more important than the restoration of an earthly temple was the establishment of a heavenly service in which Christ is our high priest and ministers daily on our behalf.

Did Daniel understand all this? Perhaps not. But it is a blessing that we, living after the time of Christ, can see how wonderfully God's purposes are working out for human salvation. With such a God, do we have any reason to face the future with anything but confidence?

PRINCIPLES OF LIFE

As we have studied the ninth chapter of the book of Daniel, would you say that the following statements are reasonable deductions?

1. The right place to find answers to our theological questions is in the Bible. Science can help us with the study of nature around us, but only an inspired book can tell us

what science can never reveal.

2. The study of the Bible will be helpful to us in the long run only as we recognize its ultimate Source and seek by prayer and obedience to understand its message for us today.

3. Confession is a good exercise, because through it we recognize what we are and how dependent we are upon God.

4. Our approach to God is valid only because of God's mercy. Apart from His mercy and grace it would be futile.

5. Just being sorry for our sins does not of itself clear us of guilt. God must cleanse us from sin if our sorrow is to be effective.

6. God wants us to understand His ways, and He is more than willing to give us light when we strongly desire it.

7. A man like Daniel is highly esteemed because he is concerned about those matters that concern God.

8. Christ is the solution to all the world's problems. The Old Testament points to Him, and the New Testament describes Him and confirms His centrality in God's redeeming purpose.

9. The process of salvation involves the elimination of all that is evil.

10. Evil leads only to pain, suffering, and death.

WORTH NOTING:

"There is no indication that Daniel was officially qualified to take upon himself this ministry of intercession. He did not belong to a priestly family, nor was he in the ordinary sense a prophet. Solomon, whose great prayer in 1 Kings 8 is often compared with that of Daniel, could claim as king to speak on behalf of Israel, but it is one of the glories of Scripture that no special permission is required for intercession on behalf of others (cf. Neh. 1:5ff.). Thanks to the study of 'the books' and the habit of prayer three times a day

(Dan. 6:10), the instructed Jew was not at a loss when he came to put his prayer into words" (Joyce Baldwin, *Daniel: An Introduction and Commentary* [Downers Grove, Ill.: Inter-Varsity Press, 1978], p. 160).

"Total lack of self-interest and deep concern for God's name, kingdom, and will characterize this prayer, which Montgomery calls 'a liturgical gem in form and expression.' His comment, 'The saint prays as the church prays,' draws attention to the importance of public prayer in shaping private devotion, and the great prayers of the Bible, including this one, provide principles which we do well to incorporate in both public and private prayer today. Above all we need to recapture the assurance that God answers prayer" *(ibid.,* p. 167).

A Vision
of Christ: Activity
Behind the Scenes

With the tenth chapter of the book of Daniel we enter upon the last vision, which will take us through chapters 11 and 12 to the end of the book. Chapter 10 is an introduction. It is not so much a revelation of the future as a theophany in which God reveals Himself to Daniel through the form of a man.

The prophet tells us that this occurrence took place in the third year of Cyrus. The authorities had already issued a decree to rebuild the Temple (Ezra 1:1-4). They gave the gold and silver vessels that Nebuchadnezzar had taken from the Temple in Jerusalem and stored in the house of his gods to Sheshbazzar, the prince of Judah (verse 8). About 50,000 of those who had been in exile, including servants, set out for Jerusalem and Judah (Ezra 2:64, 65). Once settled in their estates, they began building the altar and the Temple. When they had finished with the task of laying the foundation, they raised their voices in thanksgiving and praise to God (Ezra 3:11). "But many of the older priests and Levites and family heads, who had seen the former temple, wept aloud when they saw the foundation of this temple being laid, while many others shouted for joy" (verse 12). Apparently the people had mixed feelings during the reconstruction of the Temple.

But trouble was to come from the outside. The enemies of Judah and Benjamin asked to assist with the building, but the Jewish leaders refused their offer, and so they started a campaign of slander. "They hired counselors to work against them and frustrate their plans during the entire reign of Cyrus king of Persia" (Ezra 4:5).

We have no reason to suppose that Daniel did not know what was going on. News certainly filtered back to the captives who had remained in Babylon for one reason or another, and he was greatly concerned about the situation. The question was Would the enemy succeed in hindering the completion of the project?

Daniel was well aware of the conflict between truth and error, between the saints and those opposed to them. Not that the saints were perfect, but at least they had dedicated their lives to God's purposes, to His worship. Despite all their faults, their heart was in the right place. Daniel's visions had indicated conflict, and the vision he was about to receive "concerned a great war" (Dan. 10:1).

It is interesting to note that Daniel, as he begins the tenth chapter, identifies himself as called Belteshazzar. In so doing, he emphasizes the unity of the whole book of Daniel. He is telling us that the Daniel taken into captivity about 70 years previously is the same Daniel who is having this last vision. The prophet would now be a man in his late eighties. His age may have prevented him from returning to Jerusalem, or on the other hand, he may have felt that his influence at court was important enough for him to stay behind and support his fellow countrymen in Babylon. His intercessory prayers (cf. Dan. 9) alone were of great value. We see here that every man has his appointed place of service and that we do not all have to do the same thing in order to accomplish God's purposes.

Daniel's concern leads to fasting and prayer. He "mourned for three weeks." We must not limit our concept of mourning to the times when a loved one passes away. Instead, we should mourn when we see weaknesses in ourselves or in others, when we see God's work on earth hindered because men and women do not rise up to their responsibilities.

We can measure the seriousness of his concern by his

abstinence from those things that would give him pleasure. Sometimes we show our concern only by the words we use, and people can easily see through that. Our influence then is nil. Sometimes we fast in order to make our prayers more effective, but that puts the cart before the horse! Fasting has its place in the Christian life. Jesus said of His disciples, "The time will come when the bridegroom will be taken from them; then they will fast" (Matt. 9:15). Jesus Himself fasted in preparation for His ministry. However, one type of fasting is hypocritical, and the Christian must have nothing to do with that (Matt. 6:16-18).

It is interesting to note the time of Daniel's fasting and prayer—in the first month of the year, the month that the Jews celebrated the Passover. (See Ex. 12:1-13, 21-27, 43-49; Deut. 16:1-8). For seven days, from the fourteenth to the twenty-first day of the month, they were to observe the feast of unleavened bread, a symbol of their haste to leave Egypt. On the fourteenth day a specially chosen animal was slaughtered at twilight, and the blood sprinkled on the lintel and the doorposts. Through Moses God told the Israelites that on that night an angel would pass over; hence the name "passover." Whereas the firstborn sons of the Egyptians would be killed because they, as a people, had identified themselves with the pharaoh and the gods of the Egyptians instead of the God of Israel, the firstborn sons of the Israelites who obeyed God's instructions would not be harmed. "This is a day you are to commemorate; for the generations to come you shall celebrate it as a festival to the Lord—a lasting ordinance" (Ex. 12:14).

Thus the Passover was to be an occasion of remembrance, a festival in which they would take the blood of an animal as a symbol of their acceptance of what God had done for them. They would eat the lamb as a token of God's mighty act of deliverance. No wonder it was to be celebrated from generation to generation.

Apparently they forgot the ordinance, because we read that among Josiah's reforms was the observance of the

Passover (2 Kings 23:22, 23; 2 Chron. 35:7-9). The children of Israel had been forgetting their dependence on God, forgetting how God had saved them, and above all, forgetting the provision of a Passover lamb, by whose blood, in symbol, they could appropriate God's plan of salvation and have eternal life.

But Daniel, a devout student of the Scriptures, one who believed in following the injunction of Scripture in every detail, would no doubt remember all this. Although he was in Babylon, where the ceremony would not be enacted by many Jews, the time of the year would remind him of the occasion. He would think of the Passover not only as a memorial of God's great power in rescuing the children of Israel from their bondage in Egypt but also as a symbol of His power to deliver from exile and to complete the project of rebuilding the Temple in Jerusalem. (Note that Exekiel indicated plans to observe the Passover when the glory returned to the Temple [Eze. 45:21].)

In the New Testament the writer to the Hebrews says that it was by faith that Moses "kept the Passover and the sprinkling of blood, so that the destroyer of the firstborn would not touch the firstborn of Israel" (Heb. 11:28). Moses acted on the instructions that God had given him. He asked no questions. In simple trust he did as told. Furthermore, "he persevered because he saw him who is invisible" (verse 27). What a difference it makes when one has clear instructions as to what to do, and he follows them. How encouraging it is to know that God is on our side and to be ever conscious of His presence! Moses had direct communion with God (Ex. 33:11).

For the Christian the significance of the feast is that Christ is our Passover. Paul, writing to the Corinthians, said, "Don't you know that a little yeast works through the whole batch of dough? Get rid of the old yeast that you may be a new batch without yeast—as you really are. For Christ, our Passover lamb, has been sacrificed. Therefore let us keep the Festival, not with the old yeast, the yeast of malice and wickedness, but with bread without yeast, the bread of sincerity and truth" (1 Cor. 5:6-8).

The insights of the New Testament on the Passover would, of course, be foreign to Daniel, but the concept of obedience and trust in God, of the celebration of His power on behalf of His people, would be much on his mind. Did he wish that he could talk to God face-to-face as Moses did? He does not say. But we may be sure that he was well acquainted with the story of Moses and might well have wished to emulate him, even to having such experiences with the Invisible as the great leader had. In any case, on the twenty-fourth day of the month, with the Passover season behind him, he is with some of his associates by the river Tigris, also called Hiddekel, and the unexpected happens.

Daniel tells the story simply. "As I was standing on the bank of the great river, the Tigris, I looked up and there before me was a man" (Dan. 10:4, 5). He goes on to describe the being as dressed in linen, the type of garment worn by a priest. He had a belt of finest gold, indicating wealth and prestige, and his body was like chrysolite, a bright, transparent crystaline substance. His face flashed like lightning, his eyes were like flaming torches, and his arms and legs resembled gleaming bronze. Like the sound of a great multitude, his voice was deep and thunderous. Obviously he was no ordinary being.

Daniel alone saw the apparition. And though his companions did not observe anything, terror seized them and they ran for cover. They could not stand to be in the "presence." The prophet himself turned pale, feeling increased weakness and helplessness as he gazed upon the manifestation. Then the being spoke, and as he did, Daniel fell into a deep sleep and lay prostrate on the ground with his face downward.

Who was this being dressed like a priest and radiating dignity and power? Daniel does not tell us, but it is obvious that it is some supernatural being greater than an angel. A comparison with other parts of Scripture indicates that the experience was a theophany, a visible appearance of God to man. Isaiah says he saw "the Lord seated on a throne, high and exalted" (Isa. 6:1). It was a terrifying experience because he felt totally unworthy to see the "King, the Lord Almighty" (verse 5). Only when his mouth had been touched with a "live coal" from the altar, was his guilt removed and his sins atoned for (verses 6, 7). Only then could he hear God's call to service and respond acceptably.

Ezekiel had a vision in which he describes "the appearance of the likeness of the glory of the Lord." And when he saw it, he "fell facedown and [he] heard the voice of one speaking" (Eze. 1:28). But in the book of Revelation we find a description that closely parallels what Daniel observed (Rev. 1:13-16). John the revelator declares afterward, "When I saw him, I fell at his feet as though dead" (verse 17). It is clear that John saw Jesus in His post-resurrection aspect, just as Daniel witnessed the Son of God in His pre-incarnation aspect.

Why does God make such appearances to human beings? It is to encourage them. John was told, "Do not be afraid." Daniel was told, "Do not be afraid" (Dan. 10:12). Through such appearances we may know that God is with us, that God knows what is going on, that He is active in the political structure of the world so that His plans and purposes will come to pass. Sometimes in our humanness, we wonder whether God sees and understands. But He does! The testimony of Scripture makes it plain that we have nothing to fear when we do what is right. When Jesus said to His disciples, "And surely I will be with you always, to the very end of the age" (Matt. 28:20), it was no empty promise.

The hand of Gabriel touched Daniel and helped him rise. He told him that he was "highly esteemed" (Dan. 10:11), the second time that the prophet received this compliment (cf. Dan. 9:23). It must have been extremely reassuring. How seldom people compliment us. Maybe we do not deserve to be complimented! Often others compliment us only as a means of securing our cooperation or consent, and then we are rightly suspicious of them. But when we know that someone deserves a compliment, should we not be more willing to express ourselves than we are? Too often we wait until it is too late!

Daniel receives assurance that "since the first day that you set your mind to gain understanding and to humble yourself before your God, your words were heard" (Dan. 10:12). Nevertheless, he had prayed and fasted for three full weeks. None of us is fully aware of all that is happening around us. We often feel that God is not hearing us. It may be that the time is not yet right for God to answer, or it may be that our attitude is wrong. Let us examine the latter possibility. Why are we making our requests? Is it for selfish interests, or is it because we want to understand, to humble ourselves before God? Too often we want to manipulate God. But God is not to be a puppet. We are to let Him be God, and we are to seek humbly to work hand in hand with Him. Each one of us must let Him have His way. As we decide what ought to be done, we must be more eager to understand what God would have *us* to do.

Gabriel now tells Daniel the reason for the delay in God's response. A cosmic struggle with the prince of Persia had lasted 21 days, the same period of time that the prophet had been praying and fasting. But Michael came to his aid, and now he was free to enlighten Daniel (verses 12-14).

In those few words we receive an insight into what happens behind the scenes. Unseen forces struggle to persuade this one and that one to do what is right. "For three weeks Gabriel wrestled with the powers of darkness, seeking to counteract the influences at work on the mind of Cyrus. . . . All that heaven could do in behalf of the people of God was done. The victory was finally gained; the forces of the enemy were held in check all the days of Cyrus, and all the days of his son Cambyses" (*Prophets and Kings*, p. 572).

We are amazed that puny men can oppose and hold in check the all-powerful God. The concept is difficult fully to grasp. But it is basic to our understanding of Scripture to know that God does not force anyone's will. He has given His creation freedom of choice, and He will never violate that freedom. The evil one would like us to feel that God is a tyrant. How often He gets blamed for all the evil that takes place around us. But in the end God's name will be vindicated, and the universe will see that He is a God of love. What we are witnessing around us is the conflict between good and evil. Evil receives the opportunity to show its hand completely, and finally when everyone has made his decision for good or evil, God will bring everything to judgment, and no one will be able to say, "I was not treated fairly."

"Here is revealed the true philosophy of history. God has set the ultimate goal, which most surely will be reached. By His Spirit He works on the hearts of men to cooperate with Him in attaining that goal. But the question as to which way any individual chooses to go is entirely his own decision to make. Thus the events of history are the product both of supernatural agencies and of human free choice. But the final outcome is God's. In this chapter, as perhaps nowhere else in Scripture, the veil that separates heaven from earth is drawn aside, and the struggle between the powers of light and darkness is revealed" (*The SDA Bible Commentary,* vol. 4, p. 860).

But who is Michael, called in this chapter "one of the chief princes"? It is a Hebrew name that means "Who [is] like God?" Although Daniel does not reveal the identity of Michael, a comparison with other portions of Scripture gives us a strong clue. Jude refers to Michael as an archangel (Jude 9). Paul tells us that the voice of the archangel speaks at the time of the resurrection from the dead (1 Thess. 4:16). John in his Gospel tells us that Jesus said that "the dead will hear the voice of the Son of God. . . . Do not be amazed at this, for a time is coming when all who are in their graves will hear his voice and come out" (John 5:25-29). Thus we may equate Michael with Christ, who is the Son of God. It is He who, with all the loyal angels, is active in the struggle against the forces of evil in this world.

"Good and evil angels are taking a part in the planning of God in His earthly kingdom. It is God's purpose to carry forward His work in correct lines, in ways that will advance His glory. But Satan is ever trying to counterwork God's purpose. Only by humbling themselves before God can God's servants advance His work. Never are they to depend on their own efforts or on outward display for success" (E. G. White letter 201, in *The SDA Bible Commentary*, vol. 4, p. 1173).

Once again a heavenly visitor tells Daniel not to be afraid. "Peace! Be strong now; be strong" (Dan. 10:19). And Daniel was strengthened, so that he was able to receive the revelation that was to be made to him, a disclosure of things to come. It is interesting to note that while earthly powers contend for power and authority, another more important conflict takes place at the same time—that between truth and righteousness on one side and error and evil on the other. Kingdoms may rise and fall, but man's concern should not be with political prestige or social advancement, or even the progress of science, but that God has His way with individuals, with the church, and with the establishment of His kingdom.

PRINCIPLES OF LIFE

Here are some more propositional statements for your consideration:

1. "More things are wrought by prayer than this world dreams of." (Does that sound like a familiar quotation?)

2. History is full of accounts of wars, full of the exploits of ambitious men. But everyone has ended up in the grave. Only a man who called Himself the Son of man has overcome the tomb, and He offers His victory to all who will believe in Him.

3. All heaven is on the side of the one who humbles

himself and seeks to understand God's plans and purposes.

4. We need not be in ignorance regarding the past, the present, or the future because God has made His will known through the Scriptures.

5. By faith, absolute trust in God, Moses was able to do great things for God and His people. The same principle holds good in our lives.

WORTH NOTING:

"As a people we do not understand as we should the great conflict going on between invisible agencies, the controversy between loyal and disloyal angels" (E. G. White letter 201, in *The SDA Bible Commentary*, vol. 4, p. 1173).

"There can be no self-exaltation, no boastful claim to freedom from sin, on the part of those who walk in the shadow of Calvary's cross" *(The Great Controversy,* p. 471).

"The Christian will feel the promptings of sin, but he will maintain a constant warfare against it. Here is where Christ's help is needed. Human weakness becomes united to divine strength, and faith exclaims: 'Thanks be to God, which giveth us the victory through our Lord Jesus Christ' (1 Cor. 15:57)" *(ibid.,* pp. 469, 470).

Prophecy Without Symbols

"The prophecy of the eleventh chapter of Daniel has nearly reached its complete fulfillment. Soon the scenes of trouble spoken of in the prophecies will take place" (Testimonies, *vol. 9, p. 14*).

So far the visions of the future, whether given to Nebuchadnezzar or Daniel, have made use of symbols. In Daniel 2 we had the symbol of an image composed of various metals. Chapter 7 depicted beasts rising out of the sea, obviously symbolic since they were not animals found in the world of nature. Chapter 8 described a ram, a goat, and horns.

It may not always be easy to know how to interpret symbols, although we use them frequently ourselves. We speak of the Russian bear, the British lion, and Uncle Sam. Cartoonists portray American political parties through the symbols of a donkey or an elephant. Fortunately for us, Daniel interprets the dreams of Nebuchadnezzar, and he has an interpreter who explains to him the meaning of his own visions. We do not have to depend entirely on our own resources to unravel the mysteries of the symbols used.

The eleventh chapter of Daniel, which we are about to study, contains few, if any, symbols. We shall soon see the difference between having such metaphorical pictures and not having any at all. One conclusion we may arrive at is that it is easier to remember the symbols than to keep in mind all the intricacies of kings both north and south!

Why the change in style? One might argue that it is easier to foretell the future in terms of general symbols vague enough to allow for fulfillment in almost any eventuality. It would be an entirely different matter to be so specific in the prophecy that only a few variations, if any, would be possible. Here would be the real test of prediction!

Because of the remarkable exactness of the prophecy in the eleventh chapter, Bible scholars who do not subscribe to the supernatural claim that the chapter is history written in the form of prediction. Thus Robert A. Anderson, in his book on Daniel in the *International Theological Commentary*, argues about chapter 11: "It has been couched in the form of prediction, but it is transparently 'prophecy after the event'" (p. 142). On the other hand, John C. Whitcomb, writing on Daniel in the *Everyman's Bible Commentary*, says: "We need to be reminded today that these are genuine prophecies and not pseudographs, written after the events they describe" (p. 143).

Gleason L. Archer, Jr., in his commentary on Daniel in *The Expositor's Bible Commentary*, edited by Frank E. Gaebelein, sums up the difference between the two viewpoints in a nutshell: "Both liberal and conservative scholars agree that all of chapter 11 up to this point [verse 36] contains strikingly accurate predictions of the whole sweep of events from the reign of Cyrus (during which Daniel brought his career to a close) to the unsuccessful effort of Antiochus Epiphanes to stamp out the Jewish faith. But the two schools of thought radically differ in the explanation of this phenomenon. Evangelicals find this pattern of prediction and fulfillment compelling evidence of the divine inspiration and authority of the Hebrew Scriptures, since only God could possibly foreknow the future and see to it that His announced plan would be precisely fulfilled. To the rationalists, however, who begin with the premise that there is no personal God and that whatever superior force may govern the affairs of men leaves the human race quite free to manage its own affairs without any supernatural interference, there is no possibility of a genuine fulfillment of prophecy" (vol. 7, p. 143).

The prophecy of Daniel 11 really begins with verse 2. The division of the Bible into chapters and verses is a great convenience allowing one to refer easily to various parts of the Bible, but it was a medieval innovation, an artificial differentiation that sometimes separates closely related parts of the Bible. The first verse of this chapter really belongs to chapter 10. It seems to merely date the chapter, as is the pattern in some other chapters.

At the same time, the words of the last verse of chapter 10 are most relevant for chapter 11. Gabriel announces, "I will tell you what is written in the Book of Truth." In verse 2 he declares, "I tell you the truth." It is interesting to note that there is in heaven a record called the book of truth. We are living in an age when written records are vital for evidence and other matters. God keeps records too!

A heavenly messenger came for the support and protection of Darius the Mede. In chapter 6 we noticed the problems he faced as he sought to save Daniel from the lions' den. His decree recorded in verses 26 and 27 may have aroused considerable religious opposition. But even pagan rulers have Heaven's blessing when they do what is right according to their light.

Daniel discovered that three more kings would appear in Persia, and then a fourth who would "be far richer than all the others." History gives us the names of the three who succeeded Cyrus: Cambyses, the son of Cyrus who reigned about eight years; the False Smerdis; and Darius the Great. The fourth ruler was Xerxes, the Ahasuerus of the book of Esther. He was fabulously rich, as one may gather from the way he entertained his nobles and officials for a period of 180 days (Esther 1:3, 4). Afterward he continued banqueting for another seven days (verse 5). The furnishings of his palace were gorgeous. The vessels to serve drinks were gold, and the guests could drink without limit (verses 6-8). What Daniel noticed was that Xerxes would gain power by his wealth and would stir everyone against Greece. Unfortunately, the Greeks dealt a decisive blow to the Persian forces at Platea, in 479 B.C. How different history might have been if Greece had become a Persian province!

Verse 3 mentions "a mighty king." Commentators agree that it refers to Alexander the Great. We can see that the vision follows the same pattern in the order of powers as Daniel 2, 7, and 8. Greece comes after Medo-Persia. But Daniel 11:4 tells us that his rule will not be long, and when he dies his empire will be divided to the four winds, confirming what we read in Daniel 8. Alexander began his conquests in 334 B.C. with the Battle of Granicus, overthrew Tyre on his way to Egypt, returned victorious from Egypt, and defeated the Persians at the Battle of Arbela in 331 B.C. But he died less than 10 years later in 323 B.C. in Babylon.

From verse 5 to verse 18 we have the remarkably detailed story of the conflicts between the king of the north on the one hand and the king of the south on the other. To the north was the Seleucid Empire. In the south ruled the Ptolemaic kings. Somewhere in this chapter we may expect to see the Roman power succeeding Greece. Many commentators end the prophecy with Antiochus Epiphanes because of his hostility to the Jews. But to cut short the prophecy with him breaks down the parallel with the other prophecies of Daniel.

Adventist Bible scholars have not spoken with one voice on the point in this chapter where Rome makes its appearance as a power. Uriah Smith and Stephen Haskell interpreted the entrance of Rome with verse 14. George McCready Price placed the entrance with verse 16. Some have seen the reference to a tax collector in verse 20 as a reference to the Caesar Augustus mentioned in Luke 2:1. In this case the "prince of the covenant" mentioned in verse 22 would undoubtedly refer to the Messiah, Jesus Christ. During the reign of Tiberius Caesar, the "contemptible person" of verse 21, Jesus was crucified in A.D. 31.

Without going into the details of history, which may be

boring to many, it is obvious from even a cursory reading that verses 23 to 27 indicate struggle and intrigue. Two expressions, however, indicate that God is in control. In verse 24 we find the phrase "but only for a time," and in verse 27, "at the appointed time." God determines to what extent powers can engage in their activities. He has a timetable, and He holds to it as He works out His purposes.

The expression "against the holy covenant" (verse 28) shows the target of all the animosity. God's plan of salvation has always been under attack. Either people do not recognize Jesus for what He is, the Son of God, or they do not see His death on the cross for what it was, a vicarious atonement for sin. Legalism is substituted for an acceptance of what God has done. The Bible is not appreciated for what it is and, in some instances, is kept away from the people. The law of God is set aside, and human traditions overshadow it.

In verse 31 we find a reference to the "abomination that causes desolation." Jesus used the term, obviously quoting from the book of Daniel, to refer to the destruction of Jerusalem under Titus in A.D. 70 (cf. Matt. 24:15). But it could well apply to any power that sets itself in opposition to the plan of salvation revealed in the gospel.

Verse 33 suggests that the struggle to maintain one's faith may result in martyrdom or loss of property. The tragedy is that those who are sincere may be joined by those who are not (verse 34), leading some of the wise to stumble (verse 35). Yet they may repent and be restored to wholeness. Christian commitment is always a personal relationship with God. We are saved or lost not as groups but as individuals. Verse 35 refers once again to the "appointed time." Whatever may be the circumstances in which we find ourselves, we may know that God sees and understands and He will not permit us to face temptation above our capacity to resist.

Verse 36 seems to be a clear reference to a power similar to that described in Daniel 7:25 as one who speaks against the Most High. What a tragedy that anyone would be so brash as to oppose the truth of God! Yet sin has no limits to the evil it can cause.

Commentators recognize verses 40 to 45 as phases of the prophecy of chapter 11 that have not yet found their fulfillment. Speculation may be fascinating and rife, but we must always cling closely to the word of Scripture. We must not get carried away by fancy theories that lead to unfulfilled expectations. Disappointment can result in disillusionment, and disillusionment can cause loss of faith. We must not let anything destroy our trust in God and His Word.

What, then, should we do when we find passages of Scripture or prophecy that we do not understand? James White gave some good advice when he said, "In exposition of unfulfilled prophecy, where the history is not written, the student should put forth his propositions with not too much positiveness, lest he find himself straying in the field of fancy" (James White in the *Review and Herald*, Nov. 29, 1877, in *The SDA Bible Commentary*, vol. 4, p. 877).

Chapter 11 ends on a triumphant note for truth and righteousness: evil will come to an end without a note of sorrow from anyone. "No one will help him."

PRINCIPLES OF LIFE

After reading this chapter, would you agree that the following principles are important for the Christian?

1. The closer we approach the end of earth's history, the more urgent it is that we become familiar with the prophecies of Daniel.

2. The remarkable fulfillment of prophecy in detail is a powerful argument for the inspiration of the Word of God.

3. Only God can foretell the future, and for anyone to seek to know it by means other than the Word of God is to court deception.

4. The presuppositions we have as we approach Scripture will determine how we interpret it.

5. The fact that we encounter so many interpretations of Scripture should not discourage us from studying prophecy for ourselves.

6. The safest interpreter of Scripture is the Holy Spirit; therefore we should always begin our study with prayer for God's guidance.

7. One of the major lessons we learn from the study of prophecy is that God has a goal that He is pursuing and He will reach His goal in His good time.

8. Evil will come to an end with a finality that is irrevocable. That day will be a day of rejoicing for all those who have turned away from it and a day of doom for all those who have been fascinated by it.

9. Satan has always sought to defame God's character and to cast doubt on His plan of salvation.

10. The greatest danger to the church is the mixture of truth and error, the association of the sincere with the insincere.

WORTH NOTING:

"Let none think, because they cannot explain the meaning of every symbol in the Revelation, that it is useless for them to search this book in an effort to know the meaning of the truth it contains. The One who revealed these mysteries to John will give the diligent searcher for truth a foretaste of heavenly things" (*The Acts of the Apostles*, p. 584).

"With regard to prophecy as foretelling, the church has lost its nerve. An earthbound, rationalistic humanism has so invaded Christian thinking as to tinge with faint ridicule all claims to see in the Bible anything more than the vaguest references to future events. Human thought, enthroned, has judged a chapter such as Daniel 11 to be history written after the event, whereas God enthroned, the one who was present at the beginning of time and will be present when time is no more, may surely claim with justification to 'announce from of old the things to come' (Isa. 44:7)'' (Joyce Baldwin, *Daniel: An Introduction and Commentary*, pp. 184, 185).

"Then the End Will Come"

"Now learn this lesson from the fig tree: As soon as its twigs get tender and its leaves come out, you know that summer is near. Even so, when you see all these things, you know that it is near, right at the door" (Matt. 24:32, 33).

One day the disciples called the attention of Jesus to the Temple and its buildings. This structure, built so strongly with large, heavy stones, naturally filled them with pride. So it shocked them when Jesus responded, "Do you see all these things? . . . I tell you the truth, not one stone here will be left on another: every one will be thrown down" (Matt. 24: 2).

When the disciples were alone with their Master on the Mount of Olives, they asked, "Tell us . . . when will this happen, and what will be the sign of your coming and of the end of the age?" (verse 3). Jesus gave them an answer, recorded in Matthew 24:4-31, and then added, "Heaven and earth will pass away, but my words will never pass away" (verse 35).

However, He made one thing clear: No one will know the day or the hour when the end will come. People will be conducting their business as usual, and the end will happen unexpectedly, He told them. "Therefore keep watch" (verse 42).

With the twelfth chapter of Daniel we conclude the book, and it is not surprising that we here receive a view of those things that will take place at the end of time. We turn to it with anticipation, because we are all interested to know how the conflict between good and evil will end and what events mark the final denouement.

We have already noted that chapters 10 to 12 represent one vision. Chapter divisions may be convenient for ready reference, but they do not always suit the topic. In our present case the last five verses of chapter 11 really belong to this twelfth chapter. They deal with events still future to our own time. But they refer to places that are familiar to us: the Beautiful Land, Edom, Moab, Ammon, Egypt, and Libya. The kings of the North and the South are still engaged in battle, with a fury and determination to "destroy and annihilate many" (verse 44). One development is of interest: "He will pitch his royal tents between the seas at the beautiful holy mountain" (verse 45).

Here are events taking place in the Middle East that we must watch with care. We must be hesitant in jumping to any conclusions. But we may be sure that just as prophecy has come to fulfillment in the past, so it will in the future.

Why has not God announced a specific time when He will usher in the end? The reason is clear. Human nature being what it is, many of us would not prepare for it if we thought it was far beyond our lifetime in the future. We would procrastinate, not realizing that for each one of us the moment of our death is virtually the end of the world. Therefore we would cease to watch, assuming that the events happening around us are of no consequence. If we are never sure when the end will take place, we will remain more alert to events around us, ever comparing what we see with what Scripture reveals. To preserve our Christian experience, we must keep constant vigil, we must ever remain in touch with the Word of God.

Jesus compared this watching with the alertness of the householder who does not know when a thief may break into his house, so he is ever on his guard. "So you also must be ready, because the Son of Man will come at an hour when you do not expect him" (Matt. 24:44).

Chapter 12 of the book of Daniel begins with the words: "At that time Michael, the great prince who protects your people, will arise" (verse 1). We have already noted that Michael is Christ. He defends God's people from the power mentioned in the previous chapter, who, with great rage, sets out to destroy and annihilate many. That is why Scripture calls Michael a protector. However, that does not mean that there will not be a time of trouble for God's people. Indeed, the difficulty that they will have to pass through will be greater than at any previous period of human history.

God vows to save His people. But He has not promised to prevent suffering. Any struggle between two forces is bound to produce casualties. But in this case the outcome is not in doubt. Therefore the troubles that a Christian experiences he or she can consider as light affliction because, as Paul says, "we fix our eyes not on what is seen, but on what is unseen. For what is seen is temporary, but what is unseen is eternal" (2 Cor. 4:18).

The powers of evil have always been under God's ultimate control. They can go only as far as He permits them. In the story of Job we see how Satan had his limits—he was not to touch Job's person (Job. 1:12). Later on, God permitted him to afflict his body, though not to take his life (Job 2:6). But the time will come when everyone has made a final decision either to be for God or to be against Him, and when that moment arrives the work of atonement ends, the righteous are sealed, and God allows the devil to vent his fury as he pleases. "Satan will then plunge the inhabitants of the earth into one great, final trouble" (The Great Controversy, p. 614).

The prime objects of his attacks will be God's people. They are the ones who, in his sight, have caused the crisis, and he is determined to exterminate them. Loyal to God's law, they have refused to follow any human tradition that undermines it (cf. Matt. 15:6). Their lives of strict propriety have rebuked those who follow their natural instincts without regard for principles of morality. As Satan realizes that his remaining time is short, he attempts to deceive everyone (Rev. 12:12). Performing miracles, he goes so far as to impersonate Christ. Many will be deceived, but the people of God are not misled. They have been diligent students of the Word of God, and they will see through Satan's ruses. Soon the world will have only two classes: the deceived and the undeceived.

As the darkest hour is before the dawn, so the time of trouble precedes deliverance. The angel tells Daniel: "Your people—everyone whose name is found written in the book—will be delivered" (Dan. 12:1). We have seen that God keeps records and that they form the basis of judgment (Dan. 7:10). Everyone's name is recorded. Paul speaks of those who have their names written in the book of life (Phil. 4:3). But those who are lost do not have their names entered in the book of life (Rev. 20:15). Apparently their names have had to be erased (Rev. 3:5).

How will God's people be delivered? The divine messenger speaks of a resurrection (Dan. 12:2). Multitudes are asleep in the dust—that is, they have died. God said to Adam, "Dust you are and to dust you will return" (Gen. 3:19). This was the result of sin. But what about those who will not die before that time? Paul explains what will happen at the resurrection: "For the Lord himself will come down from heaven, with a loud command, with the voice of the archangel and with the trumpet call of God, and the dead in Christ will rise first. After that, we who are still alive and are left will be caught up with them in the clouds to meet the Lord in the air. And so we will be with the Lord forever" (1 Thess. 4:16, 17).

You will have noticed that Paul states that those who died in Christ will rise first. John the revelator describes two resurrections: one at the time of Christ's coming and the other at the end of the thousand years (Rev. 20:4-6). Those taking part in the first resurrection are the fortunate ones, because the second death has no power over them. As for those who rise after the thousand years, they are the ones Daniel refers to as coming forth "to shame and everlasting contempt."

It is now, while we have life and the opportunity to make decisions, that we must decide which group we want to be in. The writer to the Hebrews quotes an appeal from the Holy Spirit: "Today, if you hear his voice, do not harden your hearts" (Heb. 3:7, 8). "See to it, brothers, that none of you has a sinful, unbelieving heart that turns away from the living God. But encourage one another daily, as long as it is called Today, so that none of you may be hardened by sin's deceitfulness" (verses 12, 13). Sin is deceitful because it often seems right, and the prophet Jeremiah warns that the "heart is deceitful above all things" (Jer. 17:9). We are to seek first God's kingdom, then everything else will fall into place (Matt. 6:33).

Daniel goes on to say: "Those who are wise will shine like the brightness of the heavens, and those who lead many to righteousness, like the stars for ever and ever" (Dan. 12:3). What a contrast there is between being wise and being foolish! Jesus told a parable about 10 virgins. Five were wise because they made the necessary preparations to be ready whenever the bridegroom came. The other five were foolish because they let their preparedness lapse. A knowledge of the future is not to satisfy our curiosity but to enable us to make the right decisions now.

The angel then told Daniel to "close up and seal the words of the scroll until the time of the end" (verse 4). Many parts of his prophecy would not be understood until their fulfillment. We have noticed that our understanding of the book of Daniel results from the fact that we live 2,500 years after his time. We can see how history has confirmed prophecy, how the Messiah arrived according to the 70-week prophecy. The New Testament gives us many insights that illumine our understanding, for instance, of the Resurrection. Many matters clear to us would have been obscure to Daniel and his contemporaries.

"Many will go here and there to increase knowledge" (verse 4). The passage does not explain what knowledge is to increase. Is it to be of the prophecies of Daniel? If so, then the prophecy has come to pass, although parts of Daniel still remain closed to our understanding. Is it a knowledge of the world in which we live? If so, then once again the prophecy has been fulfilled, because we live in the midst of an information explosion. Some knowledge, such as increased rapidity of travel and cures for many diseases, has been helpful, but other forms, such as the discovery of the destructive capacity of nuclear energy, put us in continual danger.

The prophet describes the persons he saw by the river. The one clothed in linen reminds us that we are still in that vision that he began recounting in chapter 10. (What a lengthy vision it has been!) One of the beings asks, "How long will it be before these astonishing things are fulfilled?" (verse 6). Would Daniel have ever dreamed that time would last another 2,000 years? Could he imagine that the struggle between the powers of darkness and the children of light would continue so long? I doubt it. He was looking for a speedy solution, just as the early disciples expected Christ to return in their day. Paul had to caution some that they should not expect the return of Jesus until prophecy had been fulfilled, in particular the prophecy regarding the man of sin (2 Thess. 2:5-12).

Every generation has expected Christ to come in its day. And there is the danger that we may say, "Where is this 'coming' he promised?" (2 Peter 3:4). Perhaps we may even join the ranks of the scoffers. But Peter reminds us that time is not a factor with God. "The Lord is not slow in keeping his promise, as some understand slowness. He is patient with you, not wanting anyone to perish, but everyone to come to repentance" (verse 9). Then he adds, "But the day of the Lord will come like a thief." We must be ready at any moment. In fact, we need to "make every effort to be found spotless, blameless and at peace with him" (verse 14).

The man clothed in linen solemnly answers the question How long? "It will be for a time, times and half a time. When the power of the holy people has been finally broken, all these things will be completed" (Dan. 12:7). The vision of Daniel 7 has previously mentioned the time period in verse 25. We are seeing that the book of Daniel is a unity. One section confirms and continues another. To understand any single part we must look at all.

Daniel says he did not understand. Are we surprised? The fulfillment would be many centuries in the future, as far as he was concerned. But we also know that prophets did not always comprehend what God revealed to them (eg., 1 Peter 1:11, 12). Even the angelic hosts watch events with close interest to learn what will happen. We understand prophecy best after its fulfillment.

As a result, Daniel himself asks, "What will the outcome of all this be?" He really would like to understand, just as we are anxious to comprehend all we can. But, like us, he had to accept his limitations. The angel told him to go his way, because the "words were closed up and sealed."

The prophecy mentions two more time periods: 1,290 days and 1,335 days. Some commentators relate the 1,290 days to the 1,260-day prophecy of verse 7 and feel that both time spans end in A.D. 1798. If the 1,335 days is an extension of this period, then we reach the year 1843, a time when the Western world witnessed a revival of interest in the prophecies of Daniel. It was an era of Bible study and research, revealing much of importance to us today.

PRINCIPLES OF LIFE

Have you noticed that the following principles arise from a study of this chapter?

1. As long as the world lasts, the wicked and the good will remain, and the two groups will never see eye-to-eye.

2. The conflict between good and evil will increase in intensity as the world comes closer to the end of time.

3. The fate of the wicked and the good has never been in doubt. The wicked will be destroyed, and the good will enjoy eternal life.

4. Wisdom is knowing what the world is all about and making adequate preparations for the future.

5. We do not have to understand everything in order to have faith in God. It is sufficient that we know only what God has revealed to us.

6. The wise Christian is the one who has one eye on the prophecies and the other on the world so that he can see how God is in control and is working out His purposes.

7. The Christian has no need to fear any future eventuality because he knows that Christ is his Saviour and protector.

8. When all is said and done, it is not so much what we have achieved that gives us joy, but that our names are written in heaven. It is not what we do, but what God has done for us.

9. We have nothing to fear from what man may do to us. The most he can do is to destroy the body, but he cannot separate us from the love of God.

WORTH NOTING:

"The book of Daniel is unsealed in the revelation to John, and carries us forward to the last scenes of this earth's history" (*Testimonies to Ministers*, p. 115).

"If those for whom the Lord has done so much will walk in the light, their knowledge of Christ and the prophecies relating to Him will be greatly increased as they near the close of this earth's history" (E. G. White manuscript 176, 1899, in *The SDA Bible Commentary*, vol. 4, p. 1174).

"When men do not make God first and last and best in everything, when they do not give themselves to Him for the carrying out of His purposes, Satan comes in, and uses in his service the minds that, given to God, could achieve great good" (E. G. White letter 141, 1902, in *The SDA Bible Commentary*, vol. 4, p. 1174).

"Those who have light and knowledge are in the greatest danger unless they constantly consecrate themselves to God, humiliating self, and realizing the peril of the times" (E. G. White letter 201, 1899, in *The SDA Bible Commentary*, vol. 4, p. 1173).

"As a people we do not understand as we should the great conflict going on between invisible agencies, the controversy between loyal and disloyal angels. . . . Pray, my brethren, pray as you have never prayed before. We are not prepared for the Lord's coming. We need to make thorough work for eternity" *(ibid.)*.

Epilogue:
Daniel's God
and Ours

"O Lord, the great and awesome God, who keeps his covenant of love with all who love him and obey his commands" (Dan. 9:4).

God is great and awesome. Paul speaks of both His kindness and His sternness (Rom. 11:22). Any concept that does not recognize His awesomeness is inadequate. For God is utterly opposed to sin. No one can sin and expect to get away with it. Yet to the repentant sinner God is covenant-keeping and merciful. There is a paradox here: As sinners, we have everything to fear, but as sinners who accept God's plan of salvation, we have nothing to fear.

As we close our study of the book of Daniel, we pause to ask ourselves What was Daniel's concept of God? How close is it to ours?

It is obvious that his understanding of the Lord buoyed his spirits up and kept him faithful in difficult times. We too will likely face perplexing times in the days ahead. If we can find out what Daniel's God was like, if we can come to know Him in the same way that the prophet did, we have the recipe for success, for overcoming every trial.

Introduction

"Put your hope in God," declares the psalmist when he feels downcast and discouraged. He knows that the Lord is the only stable force in the universe, the only One in whom he can place his trust. As a human being, the psalmist has his ups and downs, moments when the future seems dark and forbidding, and the past only confirms his forebodings. He knows no one around him to whom he can go for help, so he turns to God. A last resort? Yes! But it is not a senseless decision. For God has a way of turning disappointments into joy and helplessness into courage. "Why are you downcast, O my soul? Why so disturbed within me? Put your hope in God, for I will yet praise him, my Savior and my God" (Ps. 42:5).

Daniel purposed that he would not defile himself with the king's food (Dan. 1:8). Here was something he could do in circumstances that he could not otherwise fully understand. Why had he been taken captive to Babylon when he had done no wrong? Where was God when a pagan ruler proudly helped himself to the vessels in the Lord's house? How could the Gentiles come to know and respect the true God when Jerusalem was destroyed and His people taken captive?

In such perplexing circumstances it is easy to give up on God—to give up on everything. But we must never relinquish our trust in God or cease to obey His commandments. Rather, we are to be faithful to our present duties as we seek to learn more about our God.

A. *God as God*

Daniel does not argue for His existence. For him God is a given. In this respect he follows the pattern of Scripture everywhere. He would have agreed with the psalmist when he said, "The fool says in his heart, 'There is no God'" (Ps. 14:1). The one who denies the existence of a loving and just deity because of the evil he sees around him does not know anything about God's plans and purposes. Daniel learned that evil has only a temporary existence, and the time will come when God's righteousness and goodness will be vindicated.

1. *His Names*

Often the way we address God reveals our relationship to Him. When we speak to God as our Father we are expressing a deeply personal relationship. How do you address God in your prayers, especially when you face an unexpected crisis?

Daniel first uses the Hebrew *adonai*, the equivalent of the English "lord." The name is clearly related to *adon*, which means "the lord, the master." *Adonai* has a possessive suffix and thus means "my lord." But a study of a number of Old Testament texts strongly suggests that the name *adonai* emphasizes God's rule over all the world. Isaiah, Jeremiah, and Ezekiel use this name in reference to their commission, or call, and thus the emphasis of the name is on God's rulership and the prophet's servanthood (cf. G. Kittel, *Theological Dictionary of the Old Testament*, vol. 1, pp. 61-64).

Thus Daniel probably employed the term because it followed the pattern and example of his dedicated contemporaries, and even more importantly, he recognized that God is ruler over all and he was an obedient servant. God as supreme ruler decided the fate of Jehoiakim, king of Judah (Dan. 1:2).

Daniel might well have been chagrined at the outcome of the conflict. He might have wished that it could be otherwise. But if the Ruler of the universe had made a decision, he was not going to question it. We may not always know when an event is the result of God's direct intervention, but if God permits a thing to happen, we must trust Him to work things out. One thing is certain: God never seeks to harm us, although sin has caused some terrible ravages.

The second word that Daniel employs for God is the Hebrew *Elohim*. The name would doubtless call to mind Genesis 1:1: "In the beginning God [i.e., *Elohim*] created the heavens and the earth." Acquainted with the books of Moses, Daniel knew the story of Creation. He would have noticed the plural form of the name of God and that "created" was in the singular. It would be strange if he had not detected the apparent grammatical inconsistency. The prophet believed in one God (cf. the Shema in Deut. 6:4). Could he have had an inkling of the Trinity? Perhaps he recognized in the one who appeared to him at the river Tigris (Dan. 10:4-6) a being higher than an angel. He would not have mistaken the reference to the Messiah (Dan. 9:25), the Prince, in the light of Isaiah's prophecy: "For to us a child is born, to us a son is given, and the government will be on his shoulders. And he will be called Wonderful Counselor, Mighty God, Everlasting Father, Prince of Peace" (Isa. 9:6). Certainly Nebuchadnezzar recognized in the fourth person in the furnace a being greater than an angel.

In Daniel 9:2 our author uses the name LORD—note that all the letters are capitals. This is to indicate that the Hebrew original is YHWH, the tetragrammaton, which has no vowels, now usually transliterated "Yahweh," although the American Revised Version of 1901 spells it "Jehovah." Yahweh is in a special sense the name of the God of Israel (Ex. 20:2). He is the covenant God (Ex. 6:7). Yahweh is the God who has been active in the history of the children of Israel, but He is also the supreme God, and when the Jew said *Adonai* he was referring to Yahweh. No doubt Daniel recognized Yahweh as his God, yet he uses Lord God—*Adonai ha-Elohim*—as he begins his great prayer of confession (Dan. 9:3).

2. *His Attributes*

A person's attributes, or characteristics, make him what he is. We cannot say we know a person—or know God—until we know at least some of his characteristics.

Daniel's God is active in human affairs. While He is up there, He is also down here. He has not created the world and left it to follow its own course without direction, but is very much in control in the sense that He intervenes again and again. The Lord has a plan and a purpose that He is working out, and, without interfering with man's freedom of choice and will, He determines how far and how long a person may go in a certain direction. For example, Jehoiakim had sufficiently indicated that he was determined to do evil, and God gave him into the hands of Nebuchadnezzar (2 Kings 23:36, 37; Dan. 1:2).

However, Daniel showed that even in difficult circumstances he was determined to serve God, and the Lord gave him favor in the eyes of his superiors (Dan. 1:9) and knowledge and skill so that he could serve the Lord better (verse 17). In fact, all that each one of us has is really a result of God's goodness and gifts, and it is for us to decide what we are going to do with what we have.

Nebuchadnezzar learns from Daniel that the God in heaven sees everything (Dan. 2:28). Nothing can be hidden from Him. Yahweh can bring even a forgotten dream back to memory. And God can and does reveal such secrets. For He is in touch with man, and man can be in touch with Him. The wise men of Babylon believed that the gods can never dwell among men (verse 11). But the true God can and did dwell with men and women (cf. Ex. 25:8). And now, after New Testament times, we know that "the Word became flesh and lived for a while among us" (John 1:14).

Nebuchadnezzar was a good student. Note what he learned about God in Daniel 2:47. But, like many of us, he forgot! He needed the experience of the image on the plain of Dura to realize fully that God is all-powerful. Save people from the scorching flames of a fiery furnace? That was impossible—or so he thought (Dan. 3:15) until he saw the three Hebrews step out of the flames without even the scent of scorching upon them. Now he knew of a Being of whom he had never dreamed. As a result, he made a decree that we could never accept as in harmony with the principle of religious liberty, but we can understand his motives.

Yet Nebuchadnezzar still had lessons to learn. He must know that God is the only source of everything good and humanity has no cause for pride. The ruler learns his lesson, and when understanding returns to him, he recognizes God as "the Most High," who lives forever, who reigns supreme on the earth from generation to generation. No one can oppose Him; no one can question the rightness of His course. At last Nebuchadnezzar is a child of God.

3. *His Activities*

It is difficult to separate God's activities from His character. He lives out what He is.

Perhaps the most outstanding deed of God that the book of Daniel reveals is the way He hears and answers prayer.

Here is Daniel facing death because the wise men have not been able to tell the king his dream or interpret it. His career has only just begun. Must this be the end of his life? He asks for an extension of time, and the king grants it. Now he goes to his companions in faith and suggests a session of prayer. Can you imagine with what intensity they pray, knowing what is at stake?

It is interesting to note that Daniel was concerned not only about his own life but also that the lives of the wise men of Babylon be spared. Knowing that they were not very wise and perhaps unsympathetic to the Jewish captives, would you have been concerned about their fate? Should we be concerned about everyone's welfare, regardless of our understanding of their goodness or lack of it?

In Daniel's response to answered prayer we learn another fact about God: He has a blessed name! We are not used to emphasizing names, but in Bible times a name indicated character. God's name stands for all that He is. That is why we should never take it in vain (Ex. 20:7).

In Daniel 2:21 we read that God "changes times and seasons." Some people alter things when they have no authority to do so, thus usurping the authority of God Himself (Dan. 7:25). We must always let God be God and never try to assume His role in the family or society.

Did you notice that God gives wisdom to the wise and knowledge to those who have understanding? Why is this? (See the parable of the talents in Matthew 25:14-30.) Would it be wrong to say that God expects a certain amount of initiative on our part? We are to be individuals with the power to think and to do, and not mere robots. Made in the image of God, we are to reflect His character, and the more we reflect, the more we have to reflect.

In Daniel 5:11 we find that the queen mother refers to the prophet as a man "who has the spirit of the holy gods in him." The language is pagan in style, but it does tell us of another divine activity: He will come into our lives if we invite Him, He will write His laws in our hearts if we let Him, and He will direct our ways so that our lives can be a blessing to ourselves and to everyone else. Thank God for such a God! Would you not be delighted to be a man or woman who represents God and speaks for Him? The promise is: "Ask and it will be given you" (Luke 11:9).

Did you notice that the Lord closed the mouths of the lions because Daniel believed in his God? He responds in blessings and protection to every act of faith on our part. Observe also that God wants us to stand in dignity (Dan. 10:11). Created in the image of God, we are to reflect our worth, and God respects that honor.

B. *God in Relation to Man*

It is a good thing to consider God in His self and being, but we are especially concerned how He relates to human beings. The question is an important one, especially since all have sinned and, in this sense, deserve nothing from God. What does the book of Daniel tell us about this side of God's character?

1. *His Concern for All*

One of the outstanding messages of the book is that God has concern for the welfare of all—the good *and* the bad! God has no favorites (Acts 10:34).

The captivity of the children of Judah in the days of Jehoiakim resulted from the continued wickedness of king and people. But not all the people were guilty. Some, like Daniel and his companions, had been true to God and had kept His commandments. Yet the righteous had to go with the wicked. God gave some of the righteous positions of responsibility that enabled them to continue their lives of witness. They may not have chosen to go to Babylon, but once there they could not have asked for better treatment than they received.

We do not ask to be born here or there, in this family or that, as part of one nation or another. But where we are has only minor significance. What is important is how we relate to God. If we are determined to do what is right, He will see to it that we find our appointed place in life. Even if we have to go through the experience of Job, we will find that the latter end is better than the former. We can always cast our concerns upon God, because He cares for us supremely, and He is able to provide for our every need (1 Peter 5:7).

In the book of Daniel we see God's concern for nonbelievers. God's purpose had been that the children of Israel would be a light to the Gentiles (Isa. 42:6). Unfortunately they had failed in their mission. Paul uses strong language when he says that their behavior blasphemed His name (Rom. 2:24). What God could not get them to do by missionary means, He now accomplishes at least through Daniel and his companions—by captivity.

The story of how Nebuchadnezzar gains a knowledge of the true God is a thrilling one. The wise men of Babylon also had an opportunity to see the vast difference between the God of heaven and the false gods they worshiped. Belshazzar and his princes failed to recognize how foolish it was to worship statues of gold and silver, wood and stone, to venerate mere figments of the imagination, when the God in heaven controls their destinies. He is their judge and alone can execute His judgments. The governors who came from far away to Babylon at the command of a great potentate, expecting to bow at his feet, witnessed a miracle that revealed a greater Ruler in heaven—One who could save from fire and the only One who deserved worship.

It is remarkable that even in the establishment of a great

power like the Neo-Babylonian empire, under Nebuchadnezzar, benefit came to the people. The symbol of a tree where birds could make nests, beasts could find shade, and people could obtain fruit indicates that God looks upon governments as a means of providing the needs of the governed. Only when a nation ceases to provide a real good, when it becomes turned in on itself so that it pursues only selfish interests for the rich, does it need to be discarded.

God employs every agency to accomplish His purpose. His concern extends to all because all are His creatures. God uses His church to reach out to the needy, but when it does not fulfill its function—as happened to the children of Israel—it must suffer the consequences. However, the church is the object of God's supreme regard, and this should not lead to complacency, but to greater and more grateful dedication.

2. *His Righteousness*

By referring to God's righteousness we do not mean some ethical quality that God has. Rather, we are thinking in biblical terms of an activity in which right prevails, in which a right relationship is established between God and His people. God is righteous because His judgments are true and fair. And He is supremely righteous because He has made provision for forgiveness and salvation.

The judgment scene in Daniel is most impressive. The vision portrays the Judge in terms that suggest dignity and experience. The fire around the throne and streaming from it hints at the transcendency of the Being on the throne. Also it implies the ability to consume all evil and carry out judgment upon it. The thousands who minister to the One on the throne testify to the extent of divine dominion and power. The opening of books symbolizes the keeping of records now available for all and assures us that we need have no question about the evidence brought forth. It is all documented. The judgment is necessary for a good reason: a power on earth has acted unrighteously. It has mouthed great things, claiming authority that does not belong to it. Warring against the saints, it seeks to overturn the symbol of God's righteousness and has apparently gained some signal victories. Shall wrong prevail? Thus the need of a judgment. The cosmic hearing takes place, pronouncing the verdict in favor of the saints. Truth and righteousness prevail and wrong is vanquished.

In all this we see that righteousness is not just being right—it is *doing* right. It is seeing that righteousness prevails on the earth. Righteousness reaches out to the poor and the needy. Not only does it come to the rescue of the wrongfully oppressed, but it seeks to help the orphan by being a father, to help the hungry by providing them with bread.

In this regard Daniel 4:27 (KJV) is most significant. The prophet advises the king to break off his sins by righteousness, and his iniquities by showing mercy to the poor. Thus he equates righteousness with displaying mercy to the poor.

3. *His Long-suffering Mercy*

We have seen that God's righteousness includes acts of mercy. But in the book of Daniel it is God's long-suffering mercy that the prophet seems to emphasize (cf. Dan. 2:18; 9:4, 9, 18).

Daniel and his companions prayed for mercy when they needed to know the king's dream and its interpretation. Their lives were in real danger because Nebuchadnezzar had the power to carry out his threat. The Hebrew word for mercy used here "has to do with God's tender compassion, that pity which he has for man in his weakness and misery and helplessness" (N. H. Snaith, *A Theological Wordbook of the Bible*, p. 143). All of us have known times when we are in exactly that position. We are unable to do anything about our situation and have no way to turn except to God. And that was what Daniel did, with wonderful results.

The same word appears as in part of Daniel's prayer in which he says that mercy and forgiveness belong to God

(Dan. 9:9, 18). Daniel contrasts the confusion of his people and their leaders with the mercies that belong to God. Man cannot deny that he has done wrong, that only condemnation awaits him. His only hope is in God's mercy. If only the Lord will look down in mercy on men and women who have brought upon themselves serious trouble as a consequence of their sin and now have no means of extricating themselves. They are completely dependent upon God to show mercy.

In the latter part of the prayer the prophet points out that no one has any claim on God because of any righteousness he or she may have. Daniel would agree with Isaiah that man's righteousness is as filthy rags (Isa. 64:6). Man's only hope is in God's great mercy. Only if the Lord shows pity on man and, taking the initiative, provides forgiveness and cleansing can there be salvation.

Living as we do after New Testament times, we can see how God has shown loving-kindness to all mankind. Through Jesus He has revealed His character of love. Through the cross He has demonstrated to what lengths He was willing to go to save man. In the term *Messiah*, the Anointed One, Daniel caught a glimpse of what the Lord would do for man some 500 years after his time. The vision recorded in the ninth chapter reveals that the Messiah would make atonement for wickedness, bringing in everlasting righteousness.

Thus we have seen Daniel struggling with the same problems we face today. But he has found the solution in God and His mercy. When we face times that are equally challenging, we have the example and teaching of Daniel to follow. We serve the same God, and He will open the way before us. As a result, we can press on with absolute confidence because we know that if we follow Daniel's example and look to God for wisdom and guidance and grace, He will save us, and we can be in His eternal kingdom of peace and righteousness.

DATE DUE

DEMCO 25-370